BEYOND PURPOSE

DR. JOHN W. STANKO

E✦ergreen PRESS

Mobile, AL

Beyond Purpose
by John W. Stanko
Copyright © 2007 Dr. John W. Stanko

ISBN 978-1-58169-240-2
For Worldwide Distribution
Printed in the U.S.A.

Evergreen Press
P.O. Box 191540 • Mobile, AL 36619
800-367-8203

Table of Contents

Dedication

I dedicate this book to my one and only sibling, my sister Janet Marie. This past year, Janet took a major step in her life and started sending and receiving emails. I'm so proud of her and now we are "talking" more than ever before. It's been great.

Thanks, Janet, for being a good sister and for living a life of hard work and dedication to your values. I hope that this book will help you and others be even more productive in the days and years to come.

OTHER EVERGREEN PRESS BOOKS
BY JOHN STANKO

Life Is A Gold Mine, Can You Dig It?
A Daily Dose of Proverbs
I Wrote This Book on Purpose, So You Can Know Yours
Strictly Business
So Many leaders, So Little Leadership
Unlocking the Power of Your Purpose

Foreword

The world is full of books, web sites, and motivational speakers encouraging people to find their passion, do what they love, and pursue their dreams. That is great because people certainly should do all those things. But most do not. The older I get, the more I realize the sad truth in Thoreau's assertion that "most men lead lives of quiet desperation." And while there are various theories about the root causes of that desperation, one of the most likely is the inability of most people to spend their time and energy doing something that is meaningful and fulfilling.

Why is this so prevalent? In a world where we are surrounded by posters calling us to scale mountains and change the world, why is it that so many of us continue to invest ourselves in activities and pursuits that leave us empty? I think it has to do with two things.

First, we have to bridge the gap between having a theoretical understanding of a problem and taking practical action to address it. Second, and more important still, we aren't taking a divine approach to identifying our passion, one that places us in the context of God's plan.

In this wonderful book, John Stanko addresses both of those challenges, and tears from our clutching hands the excuses that prevent us from taking the first, and second, and third steps toward becoming the people that we are meant to be. His passion for helping us find our passion is almost unbelievable. His energy for helping people he has never met discover the purpose of their lives cannot be justified or explained in any practical, worldly way. And that is exactly his point. When you find your purpose—and John has certainly found his—you work in a way that defies conventional explanation.

But be warned. This isn't one of those nice little books that you read, feel inspired by, and put on the shelf to gather dust. It is a living, daily call to action, a personal coach of sorts. Its lessons are not always easy, but what it promises is something that every person of every age and background deserves: an opportunity to transform a quietly desperate life into a purposeful, fulfilling one. May God give you the courage, wisdom, and trust to make that transformation.

—Pat Lencioni, author of:
The Five Dysfunctions of a Team
Death by Meeting
Silos, Politics and Turf Wars
The Five Temptations of a CEO
The Four Obsessions of an Extraordinary Executive

Introduction

As I write this introduction, I am drinking coffee in my hotel room in Rome, Italy. I stopped here on my way to teach on a cruise that will retrace the steps of the Apostle Paul. On the way home, I will visit a church in London to conduct some meetings, and then stay on there for a few days for some meetings and work.

Throughout this book, I'm sure that my love for travel will come through loud and clear. As I write about my travels, people tell me, "Oh, how I wish I could travel. I would love to come to Africa with you!"

My usual response is, "Why don't you? It's not like there's only one plane leaving for Africa a year and it left yesterday! Planes leave every day with empty seats. Why aren't you in one of those seats?"

It's then that I hear the usual litany of excuses. "You don't understand. I don't have the money to travel. I couldn't get off work. My children are too young. My spouse wouldn't approve. The world is a dangerous place. What would I do when I got there?" I wonder if this is what Jesus meant when He said, "For many are invited, but few are chosen" (Matthew 22:14).

My father passed away in 1996 at the age of seventy-nine. He was a great man and father, simple and hard working. When we carried his coffin to the graveside, however, it was almost too heavy for six men to carry. No, it's not what you're thinking. My father did not weigh much; it's just that we buried him with all his regrets, unfulfilled dreams, and wishes. The weight of a life unlived and unfulfilled was almost too much to bear.

I know that helped make and shape me in more ways than one. Somewhere as a young man, I listened to my father and said, "I'm not going to wait. I'm going to do what's in my heart to do. I won't let fear rule me or worry consume me."

Then I got involved in church work, and I saw the same dynamic that I had observed in my father's life. I heard people share what they were going to do "one day." When things didn't happen, I listened to people put a Christian "spin" on their lack of action or productivity. I'll give you an example. My sister-in-law Diana is a writer, and when people would meet her, they would say something like this: "Oh, I'm so glad I met you. I feel like I'm supposed to write a book. May I have your business card? You'll be hearing from me!"

Diana and I have laughed about it many times because of all the people who ever said that, only a few ever followed through. When we did finally hear from some, they would change their tune and say things like, "I've been so busy. The Lord hasn't released me to write yet. It must not be God's timing. Plus I don't know who would ever publish or read it." The result was a lot of talk, but little action.

As a pastor, consultant, and motivational speaker, I see this scenario repeated over and over again. I teach on life purpose, and many times see people find their purpose but not take steps to fulfill it. There are a variety of reasons for this, of course, but it always saddens me to see it happen. In 2001, I began writing a weekly email newsletter called *The Monday Memo.* I would tell audiences that my express purpose in writing *The Memo* was "to be in your face every Monday morning. I want to ask whether or not you know your purpose. Are you willing to pay the price to find it? Also, are you taking faith steps to see that you achieve your dreams? Do you have faith for time, using it for your highest priority activities?"

When I wrote the book, *Unlocking the Power of Your Purpose,* I addressed the issue of knowing your purpose. Now *Beyond Purpose* addresses the issue of your dreams and goals, creativity, personal development, and time management.

Here's how I recommend that you use the book you now have in your hands.

How To Read this Book

I have selected 52 issues of *The Monday Memo* from the 300 issues that I have written. These Memos were carefully selected because they met the criteria of this book and will help you be more productive to fulfill your purpose. They are short and easy to read so that you don't spend a lot of time studying productivity. I want to give you time to be productive! I have divided the book into four sections, with thirteen short lessons in each section.

In Section One, we will focus on *dreams and goals.* I want to help you identify your dreams and what is in your heart to do. Then I will equip you to set some goals so that you can stop talking and start doing.

In Section Two, we will look at the issue of *creativity.* Many people either restrict or deny their creativity, as I did for many years. These 13 chapters will help you come to grips and embrace your God-given creativity.

In Section Three, we will concentrate on *personal development.* You are the instrument that God uses to express His love and purpose on earth. You must invest some time to fine-tune that instrument, and I will walk you through some simple steps to insure that you are producing excellence.

In Section Four, we conclude with some lessons on time management. As you will learn in this section, you have all the time in the world—24 hours every day. It's what you do with those hours that will determine whether you are productive—or just wishing that you were.

An added feature in this book, which was not in *Unlocking The Power of Your Purpose,* is an Action Plan at the end of each chapter—some short recommendations of what you can do to apply the theme of that chapter to your own life. They are designed to be reflective, with some specific assignments from time to time.

Four sections each, with 13 chapters, totals 52 chapters, equal to the number of weeks in a year. This allows you some flexibility as you choose exactly how you want to use this book. Here are your options:

1. You can read through the book as you would any other book, stopping only to reflect or work on the Action Plan as you see fit.

2. You can read one chapter every week in the order in which they are written. You may re-read the chapter a few times during the week and take your time working through the Action Plan.

3. You can read one chapter per week, but not in the order in which they are written. You may pick a chapter from Section Two one week, then go back to study a chapter in Section One the next week, and move on to chapters in another section the following weeks.

The Action Plans are to get you moving and aren't intended to be a comprehensive collection of exercises for the topic at hand. Some may overlap with or repeat what others have already stated, which may be less of an issue if you choose to take one year to work through the book.

Additional Materials

I recommend that you invest in three things before you

start, if you don't already have them. The first is a journal. I would like you to record your reflections and the answers to some of the questions in the Action Plans. Even if you already use a journal for other writing or devotions, I suggest that you obtain another one and allow it to be your productivity/creativity journal. It's in this book that you will deal with issues that hinder or release your productivity. I hope you will continue to use it as such after you finish studying this book.

The second is a time-management system. I have used the Franklin Covey two-page per day system for the last 12 years. The company now sells a wire-bound Compass System as opposed to their seven-hole notebook system. I use that system at present.

Prior to Franklin Covey, I used Day-Timer. I also use a handheld device along with Microsoft Outlook on my computer. I'm not recommending one system over another, but if you wish to be productive, you need to identify a system that works for you, and then use it.

The third is a coach, mentor or accountability group. Most of us need others with whom we can share our innermost fears and inhibitions where productivity is concerned. I strongly urge that you find a supportive person or persons with whom you can share your productivity journey as you read this book. Make commitments to them and ask them to hold you accountable to your commitments. Otherwise, the business of life may cause your best intentions to become nothing more than wishful thinking.

If you simply want to read through this book as is, then you may not need anything else. Once you read through, however, you may see the value of taking more time to allow the issues of productivity—dreams and goals, creativity, personal development, and time-management—to settle in the deep recesses of your heart and mind. If that's the case, don't be in a hurry. It is worth investing one year to learn how to create the life you have always wanted to have.

Jesus said in John 13:17: "Now that you know these things, you will be blessed *if you do them*" (emphasis added). You are blessed, not if you know or talk about what you are to do; you are blessed when you do those things. John 15:16 says: "You did not choose me, but I chose you and appointed you to go and bear fruit—fruit that will last."

You can call productivity whatever you like—fruit, good deeds, life's work, or anything else that makes you comfortable—as long as that word stimulates action and not discussion. If all you want to do is talk about or debate a course of action, then this book and this author are not for you.

Are you ready to get started? I know you are. I wish I could write more, but I am on a deadline—not the deadline from my publisher, but from my tour guide in Rome. The shuttle for downtown is leaving, and I have one more day to view the wonders of Rome, the eternal city. May the Lord bless you as you read and work through these lessons, and at the end may you find new joy in creating the life you always wanted to have.

John Stanko
Rome, Italy

SECTION 1

Dreams and Goals

You will also declare a thing, and it will be established for you; so light will shine on your ways (Job 22:28 NAS).

I often ask people when I meet with them, "What do you see yourself doing next year? In five years?" Your ability to see what you want to do is the critical first step in the productivity process.

Once you see it, then you need to set a course for how to achieve it. That's where goals come in. It's important that you verbalize what you want to do and then tell others what that is. If you can't say it, then you're not ready to do it.

This section will help you to articulate your personal vision and then take steps to see it come to pass.

WEEK 1
Start Talking

When I started my public speaking career, I would tell people that Proverbs was my favorite book in the Bible. I would also tell them that "one day" I would write a book with Proverbs as its focus. People would see me after that and ask how my book was coming along. That would irritate me, and I would respond, "I haven't started. I'm busy...but how is *your* book coming along?" I wanted to talk about writing that book. In reality, I didn't know how to write it or where to start, so I put it off.

Then one day I decided that I was teaching about goals, but I wasn't doing what I was teaching. So I stopped saying "one day" and began to say, "By this time next year, I will have my book on Proverbs finished."

That was when I had the idea to do a devotional, focusing on one verse from a chapter of Proverbs for that day and developing a 250-word explanation to go with it. You know what happened? I did not finish the book in one year, but I did finish it in 15 months. Today it is one of my best-selling books.

It's important to speak about your goals. You can't do that in wishful terms or by saying things such as, "I hope to," "I would like to," or "One day I may." You have to commit yourself to do it, even if you have no idea how it can be done. An important part of the process is telling other people that you will do it and have them hold you accountable.

A dynamic is released when you tell others what you will do. I don't understand how, or why, it happens, but the verse at the start of this section describes it. Here is another verse that gives you additional perspective on why it's important to broadcast your goals to others: "Then those who feared the Lord spoke to one another, and the Lord listened and heard them; so a book of remembrance was written before Him for those who fear the Lord and who meditate on His name" (Malachi 3:16 NAS).

We are afraid to announce our goals in case we don't finish them. By keeping them secret, we don't attract the kinds of questions I got when people asked me about the progress of my Proverbs book. By not announcing them, however, we lose the creativity and accountability that our words produce. So, if you hope to fulfill your purpose, and increase your productivity and self-esteem, start talking.

ACTION PLAN: Is there something that you have said you will do "one day"? Why not consider when you think you can have it done? If you really can't say when, then why not declare, "I am going to do it as quickly as humanly possible." After you've determined what you're going to do, write these goals in your journal. And then you must let others know—not everyone, but those who can give you encouragement and support. Pick one of your goals from your journal list and tell (or write) three people this week to let them know what you're going to do.

WEEK 2:

What Do You See?

I travel to Africa often, spending much of my time in the beleaguered nation of Zimbabwe (the country formerly known as Rhodesia). Life is challenging in Zimbabwe. It has one of the world's highest rates of HIV infection and death from AIDS. This, along with economic downturns, high inflation, currency devaluations, and other social problems makes life extremely difficult there.

You would think that teaching on dreams and goals could be challenging in a country like Zimbabwe. But if the principles I'm teaching you are valid, they should be valid anywhere on earth, no matter what the circumstances. While teaching in Zimbabwe recently, I asked all the participants to close their eyes and focus on something they wanted to do with their lives. By doing this, I was trying to put them in touch with their dreams. To my surprise, every man and woman there saw something, and they got excited telling me what they saw. One man saw himself performing on stage, while another envisioned himself speaking before 50,000 employees—from his own company! One woman saw herself running a totally different business than the one she was currently leading; another had a vision of herself driving a sports-utility vehicle that she was able to purchase while she led a successful consulting firm. Others saw themselves and their families on vacations in places like Europe or the United States.

I was reminded in that seminar that everyone has some dreams, and that includes you. No matter how bad conditions may get, the dreams stay alive. In fact, those dreams will actually sustain and nurture you during tough times. That's why it's so important that your dreams stay alive and that you regularly take some steps to see them fulfilled, no matter how simple those steps may be.

There is something you can do this week to bring you a step closer to your dreams. It all starts, however, with seeing them and keeping them alive in your mind's eye. Are times tough for you right now? Don't forget your dreams! For example, when I close my eyes, I see myself speaking before large audiences of 20,000 or more. So what can I do this week to help further that dream? I could watch and study the techniques of a speaker on television who is addressing a large crowd, watching his mannerisms or studying her style. Even if I never speak to those large crowds that I "see," my working toward that will make me a better communicator to the crowds I do address. So nothing will be lost this week as I improve my skills in front of no one in particular.

This entire process depends on you using your God-given ability to visualize. Once you see yourself doing something, then go rehearse doing it again and again in your mind. While you're at it, see yourself impacting a lot of people when you do it. After all, it's no harder to speak to 1,000 than it is to 100 people. It's no more work to write knowing that 1,000,000 will read it than it is if it's read by a class of 25 people. I hope you get my point. You have to see yourself doing something before you can do it. Once you see it, then doing it becomes a matter of time.

ACTION PLAN: Perhaps you don't think you have the ability to visualize. Let's try something fun then. Close your eyes and visualize your ideal house. Where would you like to live?

What does the entrance look like? The exterior of the home? Visualize the various rooms, such as the living room and kitchen. What other features can you see? Be as detailed as you want, including furnishings, wall hangings and wall colors. Don't be in a hurry to finish. Go back and revisit the house more than once this week. Then find one person to whom you can describe this house. If you don't have anyone to tell, then write it (or draw it) in your journal—something you may want to do anyway even if you do tell someone.

WEEK 3

Stop It!

A few years ago, my family and I enjoyed a wonderful visit to London. We saw many of the famous sites, took in a London show, and did a lot of window shopping. I even had the opportunity to preach and teach at Spurgeon's Seminary, named after the famous British preacher of the nineteenth century. I felt smarter just being there, and I need all the help I can get!

Anytime I travel, I take several books with me to read and study. Since I was focusing on my creativity during that trip, I took *The Artist's Way* by Julia Cameron. The subtitle of this book is "A Spiritual Path to Higher Creativity." The stated purpose of the book is to provide a course in discovering and recovering one's creative self. I recommend the book as a comprehensive guide to help you develop the disciplines necessary for creativity.

There are many tips throughout the book to help you unblock and release your creativity. One section focuses on things to stop telling yourself. Some examples are:

- Stop telling yourself, "It's too late."
- Stop waiting until you make enough money to do something you'd really love.
- Stop telling yourself, "It's just my ego" whenever you yearn for a more creative life.
- Stop telling yourself that dreams don't matter, that they are only dreams and that you should be more sensible.
- Stop fearing that your family and friends would think you are crazy.

• Stop telling yourself that creativity is a luxury and that you should be grateful for what you've got.

Cameron continues, "As you learn to recognize, nurture, and protect your inner artist, you will be able to move beyond pain and creative constriction. You will learn ways to recognize and resolve fear, remove emotional scar tissue, and strengthen your confidence. Damaging old ideas about creativity will be explored and discarded."[1]

The issues she raises are critical if you are going to find a purposeful and productive life. You must learn to trust what God, who is the source of all creativity, has put in you. How many excuses do you have that serve to restrict your creativity? Are you ready to confront those excuses and remove them from your creative inventory? I urge you to put Cameron's book on your to-read list as an important aid for your creative productivity.

ACTION PLAN: Do any of the above statements apply to you? As you approach this week, examine your own attitude towards creativity. Is your definition of creativity restricted to artists and writers? Maybe your creativity lies in other areas. Do you like to build with wood or metal? Are you an inventor or business person who sees creative new ways to approach age-old problems? Are you good with money and investing? You may have an idea for a house you've always wanted to design and build, or maybe an idea for a business. Or perhaps you are a seamstress, a cook, or a baker with new designs and ideas.

Whatever the expression of creativity that is yours, what are you prepared to do about it this week? If nothing else, you may have to take steps to overcome your bias regarding creativity and go to the kitchen or workshop and get your hands dirty.

WEEK 4

How Did I Get Here?

Another time I was in London by myself, walking the beautiful streets, trying to figure out how in the world I got there. I understood that I had gotten on a plane and flown there, but that's not what I'm talking about. I'm thinking about how God worked out all the circumstances to allow my life to intersect with the lives of people in far flung places.

I first taught about life purpose in 1991 as an experiment, testing the message in a workshop to see if anyone was interested. I've gone on to conduct that workshop almost 1,000 times in more than 20 countries. Then I visited Zimbabwe in 1995 for one day—or so I thought—only to have my passport stolen. I ended up staying three more days, and I've since been back too many times to count. What seemed like an unfortunate incident turned out to be a fortuitous one that has opened many doors for me to impact a nation, and to be impacted by it.

There are many other stories I could tell that would help you further understand "how I got here." I will choose just one part of the story that I want to look at this week. My journey to do what I am doing today started with a dream. For you to get to where you want to go will start with a dream, too.

As a child, I can remember looking up in the sky and seeing an airplane. I had studied the logos and designs of the various airlines, so I saw the plane in the sky and knew to which airline it belonged. Another childhood pastime was stamp collecting. I would get piles of foreign stamps, organize them, and then study a world map to see where that country was. Ironically, my family never traveled anywhere, nor did we ever take a family vacation away from home. So I dreamed of one day traveling, being on one of those planes that I saw in the sky, going to one of the places represented in my stamp collection.

Many years later, I discovered that my purpose was to create order out of chaos. I "saw" myself speaking to crowds, sometimes large crowds, and they were smiling and laughing. Whatever I was telling them, I knew they were enjoying it! Then I had this strong sense that I would be going to Africa. So I began to study the map of Africa, wondering where I would go. All the while, I was working to develop my message and improve my ability to communicate. Finally, my employer sent me on a business trip to South Africa in 1993, and I've been going back ever since—today representing my own company.

I'm now more than 55 years old, but I still have dreams. For instance, I would like to write a book that a lot of people read and find helpful. I can see them smiling and shaking their heads in agreement as they read. I can also see them recommending the book to their friends. I would love to organize one big conference before I die—I'm talking about a huge conference with 50,000 or more participants, preferably over a two- or three-day period.

I would also like to be part of a creative team that produces something significant, that touches many people's lives all over the world. For example, when I watch the movie *Titanic*, I marvel at how well it was written and conceived. When I watch it, I pray, "Lord, I'd like to be part of a team that could create something like that for You!" I would also love to lead that team, but I would do it in a low-key way, emphasizing *team* rather than *my position*.

Finally, I would really enjoy having a regular media show, either on radio or television. I would speak some, but would also take calls and answer questions. I would interview people and let them shine, similar to how Larry King does. What little media I've done has been satisfying, and people have told me I'm good at it. Every proposal or attempt to do this on a regular basis, however, has not gone very far to date.

Now I've told you my dreams; how about discovering yours? Dreams are an important part of fulfilling your purpose and being productive. They put you in touch with your heart, and they take you out of the rational world to a world of vision and adventure. They enable you to escape your limitations and give you energy to do what you didn't think you could do. I've shared some of my dreams with you to stimulate your creativity and boldness, so that you can articulate yours.

Get out of your everyday world for just a few minutes this week and enter the world of what could be. Who knows, in a few months or years, you may be writing to someone like I am writing to you now, telling them about how you got to where you are. When you do, you will tell them what I've told you today—that it all started with a dream.

ACTION PLAN: This week, ask yourself the question, "What are my dreams?" Transfer those dreams from your heart to your journal. Now look at them and see how you can turn them into goals. Study them and see if there is anything you can do this week, no matter how simple, that could bring you one step closer to achieving one of your dreams.

WEEK 5
Daydreams

Recently I was on a plane after a long day of work. I was tired, and everything in me wanted to rest or just look at the magazine in the seat pocket in front of me. I looked at my to-do list, however, and pulled out my computer to write. I had just a few days to finish writing a Bible study, and there was much work to do. What was the key to help me ignore my fatigue and spend an hour finishing the study?

There were three things that helped me. First of all, I had it written down to do. Every day I try to make a prioritized to-do list. Such simple things as prayer, reading, and writing are always on that list. I'm not saying that I do all those things every day, but I can't ever say I forgot to do them because they are in my face, written by my own hand. Second, I have made commitments. Right now there are 6,000 people waiting every week for my Bible studies. That's a lot of people to disappoint. Third, I have a big dream and I have a goal to see that the dream becomes a reality.

For 15 years I've said to myself, "I would like to write Bible commentaries one day." In August 2001, I took a step toward fulfilling that dream when I published *The Faith Files*, a study of faith in the New Testament. After that I set an ambitious goal: To finish a devotional commentary on every book in the New Testament. I've broadcast this goal to anyone who will listen, and announcing it, in my opinion, is an important part of completing it. That goal now guides my daily activities, and writing had better be part of those activities or that goal is nothing but a dream.

T. E. Lawrence, who is perhaps better known as

Lawrence of Arabia, said these words about the power in a dream that turns it into a goal:

> All men dream: but not equally. Those who dream by night in the dusty recesses of their minds wake in the day to find that it was vanity: but the dreamers of the day are dangerous men, for they may act their dreams with open eyes, to make it possible.

I want to change the world, or at least my world. Doing that hinges on my ability to pull out my computer, some nights at 8:30 p.m., to write when I could be doing something else. I pray that you will learn how to do the same, or else your dreams will remain simply dreams.

ACTION PLAN: Isn't it time you transfer your dreams from the night to the day? Isn't it time to fill those idle moments with some activity of purpose, some activity that is close to your heart? Identify and then clarify a dream that you have, that you said you would do "one day." Once it is clear, I want you to find three people with whom you can share your dream-turned-goal. If you don't have anyone to tell, then write and tell it to me at johnstanko@att.net.

WEEK 6
Out of the Shower

Failure is a great teacher (we'll discuss that more in the coming weeks). It teaches us what not to do and what we can do better the next time. Failure is your friend but is easily considered an enemy, something to avoid and not discuss openly. I learned so much during a season when I traveled and did *Seven Steps of a PurposeQuest* seminars. Much of what I learned was *how not to do* seminars.

When you pay attention, you can find many profound quotes about failure from great leaders. Perhaps you need to be reminded this week that your failures have been painful but not fatal. What's more, there's no way you can avoid more of them, not if you're serious about being purposeful and productive. Let's look at some great quotes about failure:

Sometimes we will fail more than we succeed, but if we fail to succeed due to fear of failure, then failure becomes our success. —*Unknown*

Success is going from failure to failure with great enthusiasm. —*Winston Churchill*

Success is simply the exertion and utilization of an entire series of failures. —*Dr. Bruce Ogilvie, sports psychologist*

There are no secrets to success. It is the result of preparation, hard work, and learning from failure. —*Colin Powell*

Failure is not the worst thing in the world; the very worst thing is not to try. —*Unknown*

There are costs and risks to a program of action, but they are far less than the long-range risks and costs of comfortable inaction. —*John F. Kennedy*

There's one more quote that I like, from businessman Nolan Bushnell. He said, "Everyone who's ever taken a shower has an idea. It's the person who gets out of the shower, dries off and does something about it who makes a difference." Is it time this week to get out of your shower, dry off, and get back in the game? Has failure, or the fear of it, caused you to take off your uniform, so to speak, and sit in the grandstands as a spectator? If so, then you need to do some work to better understand the role of failure in your life. I'll be glad to help you do that.

ACTION PLAN: Which of the failure quotes above means the most to you? What does it say to you about your life and situation? Go to www.google.com and spend five minutes researching what others have said about failure. Keep a section in your journal about failure in general, your failures, and the lessons you've learned from your failures.

15

WEEK 7
"I Hate You, John Stanko"

I talk to many people who are unhappy in their jobs. Most of them feel trapped and don't see any way out of their dilemma because they have bills to pay and families to feed. One man told me half-jokingly, "I hate you, John Stanko! Where were you 20 years ago when I gave up my dream? Now I am in a job I hate, but I have a mortgage and school bills to pay. What can I do?"

The answer for this man was to reconnect with his dream of 20 years ago. As he took steps to do so, he kept his job but he also published a novel and produced several music projects that were recorded and distributed for sale. I think, in due time, he will be able to transition from the job he hates to one he loves. I am seeing that happen more and more.

Solomon summarized his search for wisdom when he wrote:

> *So I conclude that, first, there is nothing better for a man than to be happy and to enjoy himself as long as he can; and second, that he should eat and drink and enjoy the fruits of his labors, for these are gifts from God* (Ecclesiastes 3:12-13 TLB).

Solomon practiced what he preached. Here is a report from the visit of the Queen of Sheba to Solomon's court:

> *When the queen of Sheba heard how wonderfully the Lord had blessed Solomon with wisdom, she de-*

cided to test him with some hard questions.... Solomon answered all her questions; nothing was too difficult for him, for the Lord gave him the right answers every time...She also saw the beautiful palace he had built, and when she saw the wonderful foods on his table, the great number of servants and aides who stood around in splendid uniforms, his cupbearers, and the many offerings he sacrificed by fire to the Lord—well, there was no more spirit in her!

She exclaimed to him, "Everything I heard in my own country about your wisdom and about the wonderful things going on here is all true. I didn't believe it until I came, but now I have seen it for myself! And really! The half had not been told me!...Your people are happy and your palace aides are content—but how could it be otherwise, for they stand here day after day listening to your wisdom! Blessed be the Lord your God who chose you and set you on the throne of Israel" (1 Kings 10:1-8 TLB).

This story intrigues me because of the queen's summary of her visit. Solomon was functioning in his purpose (wisdom), and she consequently saw that the people around him were happy! What she saw led her to break out in praise, praise to a God whom she did not serve. When was the last time someone broke into worship because of the job they saw you doing? When was the last time someone was impressed with the joy and contentment they saw in you and the people with whom you are working?

You cannot produce innovative, creative, and exceptional results unless you and the people around you are doing what you love. Why don't you think you're entitled to that kind of joyful work? Why don't you take the time to find out why you aren't happy so that you can produce extraordinary work and bring glory to God, even among those who don't know Him? This takes great courage, for often others will tell you that you are crazy or that it isn't possible!

If you ask me what I would do if I had all the money I needed, I would answer that I would do what I'm already doing. I've made difficult decisions in the past that have enabled me to do what I love today. The results, I believe, indicate that I'm doing what I love. Why don't you follow this example and take steps today that will enable you to do what you love tomorrow?

ACTION PLAN: Are you producing excellence or are you just getting by? Are you doing what you love and loving what you do? What would you do if you didn't need the money? What would you spend your time doing? If you don't answer that you would stay in your current job, then why are you there now? What can you do over the next five to ten years that would enable you to do the work you love? Write it down in your journal.

WEEK 8
A Shirt Tale

Last week, we looked at Solomon and the excellence he produced. Have you ever tried to define excellence? I have, but my definition has changed over time. In the past, I defined excellence as perfection and consequently found myself frustrated most of the time because I seldom achieve perfection. I've come a long way in my thinking on this subject, however, and I no longer equate excellence with perfection.

So how do I define excellence now? To answer that, allow me to tell you a happy story that still shapes my life and thinking about excellence. In 1986, our family was on vacation in the San Francisco area. On New Year's Eve, we went shopping at a local mall and went to Nordstrom's, a department store famous for its service. I bought four dress shirts there, and then my family split up to do some more shopping. My wife and daughter went one way; my son and I, the other.

When we met again, the first thing my wife asked me was, "Where are your shirts?" I realized then that I had put down the bag somewhere in the mall and had forgotten to pick it up. We quickly retraced my steps, which eventually led us back to the counter where I had purchased the shirts. I explained my dilemma to the sales people, and they were empathetic. One of them said, "Why don't you pick out four more shirts?" I explained that I could not afford four more shirts, but she insisted that I identify the shirts I had lost. Two other sales assistants joined us as we found the four shirts in my size.

19

Then the sales person put those shirts in a bag and said, "Happy New Year from Nordstrom's. There's no additional charge!" I was astounded! They had replaced my shirts free of charge. I went on to write an article about that experience for a magazine, and I entitled the article, "A Shirt Tale."

That story is the best definition of excellence I've ever experienced. It taught me that excellence is an attitude that goes beyond the call of duty. It also taught me that excellence is not defined by the doer, but by the receiver. I doubt that the sales people who gave me my shirts remember what they did, but I will never forget it. It took my breath away.

Are you a person of excellence? If so, when was the last time you took someone's breath away when they encountered your commitment to go beyond the ordinary? This kind of excellence can't be learned; it can only come from doing what you love while serving others. What's more, doing what you love, with excellence, is a tremendous source of energy, enabling you to fulfill your purpose by being more productive. I hope that this week you can impact someone's life as they encounter your purposeful excellence.

ACTION PLAN: What is your definition of excellence? Do you have a favorite story that would be a great example of excellence? What can you do to "take someone's breathe away" in your work or ministry? In what area are you most committed to excellence? Keep an excellence section in your journal and record any examples of excellence (or non-excellence) that you encounter in the week to come. Make sure you write how those examples made you feel.

WEEK 9

Pressed for Time

My wife's 83-year-old father passed away a few years ago. He lived in Maryland, and as soon as we received word, Kathryn, of course, left immediately to be with her mother, sisters, and brother. I stayed behind for a few days for I had some juggling to do if I was going to go to the funeral.

First, I had to reschedule my flight to London from Thursday to Friday night. Then I had to attend to everything I needed to get done and pack my things by Wednesday so I could drive down to Maryland. I had to pack not only for my trip but also for a funeral. During this time, I kept in constant touch with Kathryn to see how she and the family were doing.

The funeral was a small affair with mostly family and a few friends. My father-in-law was a good man, who worked hard, enjoyed his retirement, loved his family, and served God as best he knew how. It is unfortunate that it takes a funeral to bring together a family that lives all over the country, and it was quite good to see everyone, even though our hearts were heavy.

After the funeral, I raced to Dulles Airport in Washington, D.C., for the flight to London. I arrived in London at 7:00 a.m. and was taken to my hotel so I could take a quick shower. I went directly to the church where I spoke at a leadership conference. Then it was back to the hotel for a quick nap, after which I returned to the church to speak at the evening session. I got back to the hotel about midnight that night, grateful that we turned the clocks back that night, and got an extra hour's rest. On Sunday I spoke at the morning and evening services, and got up at 3:30 a.m. to catch a flight to Nairobi, Kenya.

I'm neither bragging nor complaining when I report these things to you. I've found that I don't always know what I can do until I have to do it. I wasn't sure whether I could fit in everything during that hectic week, but with God's help, I did.

Some of the events, like the funeral, were not in my planner at the beginning of the week. I didn't have anything to do with those events occurring. Other events I planned and had a hand in creating. Both provided important incentives to do what I did. Let me explain.

My father-in-law's death created urgency in my life that caused me to maximize every minute. I had to plan my work and work my plan if I were going to prepare, pack, drive, and then fly to London. I had no time for frivolous activity, and the goal of attending the funeral helped me stay focused. Then I had another goal of being in London, and that goal gave me added incentive to keep my eye on the future and prepare for something beyond the funeral.

You must set goals because things like funerals, emergencies, and the unknown will always occur, usually without warning. If you're not careful, you can use those as never-ending excuses not to produce. "I'll do that after I rest," "I'll do it next month when I have a few days off" or "I'll get to that when I retire." Truth is, conditions are seldom "just right" for setting and achieving goals. So if unexpected things are inevitable, then you need to set goals for what you expect and want to happen. When you set a goal, the unexpected can't sidetrack you for very long. After you've attended to the urgent, you can redirect your attention to the important, to the object you need to achieve as a result of the goal.

ACTION PLAN: Read and study Philippians 3:14 for the next seven days. Look at it in different translations. Write in your journal what you learn from that verse about setting goals. Jot down some goals you would like to set and achieve in the coming months. Whatever you do this week, I hope you will determine not to allow the unpredictability of life to keep you any longer from doing what is in your heart to do.

WEEK 10

Press On

Why do you need to set goals? Why can't you just float along with the tide and go where the Spirit and life lead you? The main reason is that there are too many factors working to prevent you from accomplishing what is in your heart to do. You must cooperate as you help create the life you would like to lead. Paul outlined the dynamics of a goal in the verse that I suggested you study last week. That verse states, "I press on toward the goal for the prize of the upward call of God in Christ Jesus" (Philippians 3:14). Here are some thoughts on that verse:

I press on. This tells us that there's something pressing against you, and you must exert greater force on it than it is exerting on you if you are to make any progress. What are some of the things pressing against you? Such things as laziness, fear, time and money constraints, confusion, and doubt, just to name a few. Feel free to add your own ideas to the list. Whatever you do, don't allow those forces to press you and keep you where you are. Set a goal and then press through your opposition.

For the prize. A goal has a reward—achieving something that you want to do. Reaching the goal is the prize and there's nothing wrong with working hard to win the prize. The value of the prize is enhanced when the obstacles you overcome are significant. Someone once wrote, "There's no thrill in easy sailing when the skies are clear and blue; there's no joy in merely doing things which any one can do.

But there is some satisfaction that is mighty sweet to take, when you reach a destination that you thought you'd never make."

Is upward. A goal takes you closer to God and godliness. As you struggle in faith to achieve your goal, that struggle develops something in you like exertion develops a muscle. You grow when you set a goal and make it, and the growth is almost as good—if not better—than the achievement. Many people have told me that my writing and speaking have blessed them, but I've gained much more than I've given. I've learned about God and myself in the process and now I'm better equipped to serve Him. Don't stand around with your feet on the ground. Soar to great heights by setting and achieving some goals!

Involves a call. A goal represents a desire of your heart, something that God put there in the first place. When you acknowledge that the desire is there, you honor Him by recognizing that God is the caller, and you are the called—you are simply responding to His will and initiative. Many people get hung up asking, "How do I know that this is what God wants me to do?" I always respond, "How do you know it *isn't?*" Then I quote Proverbs 16:3 from the Amplified Version: "Roll your works upon the Lord [commit and trust them wholly to Him; *He will cause your thoughts to become agreeable to His will*, and] so shall your plans be established and succeed" (AMP, emphasis added). If your heart is set to do God's will before you know what it is, then God will direct your thoughts into the paths He has for you. What a great promise!

Continue to meditate on Philippians 3:14 to see if you

get any more insight into the role of a goal. Don't be content just to study goals, however. I urge you to set some goals. Better yet, don't stop until you achieve some.

ACTION PLAN: This week identify some things you would like to accomplish in the areas of work, ministry, family, finances, and personal development. Don't get too formal yet; just jot down some ideas. There's no wrong way to set a goal so don't worry just yet about putting a date by which you want to complete everything. Simply focus on what you want to do. Write these things in your journal or on small index cards. Carry them with you, refer to them, and read them to yourself. Look at those things and be convinced they are something you truly want. Then put them in a format that says, "I will write a book and have it finished by November 30 this year" or "I will finish my college degree by this time next year." There's no wrong way to do this, but it is wrong not to do it. So get busy and set some goals! It's the spiritual thing to do!

WEEK 11

Down Time

God knows how to prepare His workers for their work. There always seems to be an element of suffering, misunderstanding, and even failure, before there is the breakthrough success that God has for His servants. This timeless principle applies to you as much as anyone else. The Bible and history itself contain many examples of this truth. Daniel is also a perfect example of this principle.

Daniel had distinguished himself in the court of Nebuchadnezzar, king of Babylon. His exploits are described in the first four chapters of the book that bears Daniel's name. When Nebuchadnezzar's son Belshazzar took the throne, we have the well-known story from which we get the oft-used phrase "the handwriting is on the wall." I urge you to read the book of Daniel, or at least chapter 5, for I will now quote from only part of that story:

> *Then all the king's wise men came in, but they could not read the writing or tell the king what it meant. So King Belshazzar became even more terrified and his face grew more pale. His nobles were baffled. The queen, hearing the voices of the king and his nobles, came into the banquet hall. "O king, live forever!" she said. "Don't be alarmed! Don't look so pale. There is a man in your kingdom who has the spirit of the holy gods in him. In the time of your father he was found to have insight and intelligence and wisdom like that of the gods. King Nebuchadnezzar your father— your father the king,*

I say—appointed him chief of the magicians, enchanters, astrologers and diviners. This man Daniel, whom the king called Belteshazzar, was found to have a keen mind and knowledge and understanding, and also the ability to interpret dreams, explain riddles and solve difficult problems. Call for Daniel, and he will tell you what the writing means" (Daniel 5:8-12).

My question to you is this: If Daniel had been so successful serving Nebuchadnezzar, why didn't Belshazzar know who he was? Why did the queen have to remind the king that Daniel even existed? The answer is simple: After his long success, Daniel now faced a down time in his life. He was forgotten, retired and rejected by the new leadership! Daniel was famous one day and forgotten the next.

While man had forgotten Daniel, God had not. The same is true for you. It may seem like all your doors are closed and that the success you once enjoyed has now evaporated into thin air, never to return. Or you may feel like you are at the end, not able to go on another day. As with Daniel, your best days may yet be ahead of you. After Daniel gave the king the bad news of what the writing on the wall meant, Daniel was once again restored to prominence:

Then at Belshazzar's command, Daniel was clothed in purple, a gold chain was placed around his neck, and he was proclaimed the third highest ruler in the kingdom (Daniel 5:29).

What should you do if you are in a season of "un-use," disfavor, or inaction? I would urge you to do three things if you are discouraged, disillusioned, or dismayed. And if you're not, I urge you to find someone who is—you shouldn't have to look too hard—and encourage them in their dark time.

Renew your faith in God. Your productivity doesn't depend on your faithfulness; it depends on God's. Remind yourself that God can do anything, and then rest in Him. Perhaps Daniel thought it was all over for him. Yet God helped him, and He will help you, too.

Keep preparing for your day of success. I don't think Daniel went home and stopped seeking God. You must keep on writing, reading, learning, and practicing. When the phone rings or the mail comes announcing your opportunity, you'll be fresh and prepared, having worked in faith for the day of success.

Be generous. Daniel was snubbed and ignored and could have refused to render his wisdom services for Belshazzar. What can you do for someone else, even though you are down and out?

Are you down and out? Then it's just a matter of time before you're up and coming, no matter how old you are or what you've been through. Learn the lessons that Daniel has to teach and write your own success story. Your most productive days are in your future, not your past. Armed with that truth, I encourage you to keep on developing for the days that are yet to come.

ACTION PLAN: Where do you want to be in five years? Don't tell me, "Wherever God wants me to be!" That sounds spir-

29

itual, but it's a cop out. What is your vision for your future? What do you see yourself doing? Write it down in your journal. Now, what steps do you need to take today so that you can prepare yourself for tomorrow? I work with a college whose enrollment is primarily adults, and a 62-year-old woman recently registered for classes. Don't tell me it's too late for you to achieve something. Get busy this week preparing for your future. A good way to do that is to visualize your future so that you know what to get ready for.

WEEK 12
Hit It Hard and Wish It Well

Years ago when I lived in the southern United States, I played a lot of slow-pitch softball in a church league. Softball is a game similar to American baseball, but the ball is bigger and the pitcher throws it more slowly and underhand. I was a pretty good player, and my team won more games than we lost. There was one team that was very good (although they didn't look as sharp as we did because we got new uniforms almost every season). Year after year, they just about always beat the teams from our church. We practiced weekly, yet we never saw them on the practice field. They just knew how to win.

One night we met some of their players on the practice field and decided to see if we could garner the secrets of their success. We asked many questions, but then our coach asked their best batsman, "When you're at bat, do you have an offensive philosophy? Do you try to hit it over the fence or do you try to advance the runners?" The man gave our coach a surprised look and answered, "We don't have any philosophy. We just hit it hard and wish it well."

As you seek to fulfill your purpose and be productive, this may be the best strategy you can follow. You may simply need to "hit it hard and wish it well." In softball, sometimes you can do everything just right and not get to first base. Other times you can do things wrong, but the ball falls in the right spot, and you win the game for your team. Perhaps you're waiting for perfection before you try something, or you're frustrated that you have done everything correctly and things haven't worked out. This week you need to overcome your hesitancy and discouragement and go to bat one more time. This hit-it-hard-and-wish-it-well principle is actually mentioned in the Bible. The writer of Ecclesiastes wrote a long time ago:

> *If clouds are full of water, they pour rain upon the earth. Whether a tree falls to the south or to the north, in the place where it falls, there will it lie. Whoever watches the wind will not plant; whoever looks at the clouds will not reap. As you do not know the path of the wind, or how the body is formed in a mother's womb, so you cannot understand the work of God, the Maker of all things. Sow your seed in the morning, and at evening let not your hands be idle, **for you do not know which will succeed, whether this or that, or whether both will do equally well*** (Eccl. 11:3-6, emphasis added).

What creativity are you afraid to express? What can you do to get out of the rut you are in? It may be something as simple as trying again. You may strike out, but you also may hit a home run. I hope that this week brings you closer to the fulfillment of what is in your heart to do and be.

ACTION PLAN: Take some time to find a sporting event on television this week. Whether it's soccer, basketball, cricket or baseball, watch the players to see how they handle failure. What do they do when they miss a swing or a kick, or shoot an errant basketball? What did you learn? Now think about what you've wanted to do, but have put off because you were afraid it wouldn't turn out as you wished? Is there some failure in your past that has caused you not to play the game, so to speak? Write those things in your journal. Now what can you do this week to restore your confidence and faith?

WEEK 13
A Box of Mints

Every year I prayerfully choose one seminar or conference to attend to help me be productive. Last year, I was in Seattle attending a seminar sponsored by The Pacific Institute when the speaker said, "We don't know how to hold onto our successes. We let go of them too quickly." I didn't know what he meant, but then he had us do two simple exercises that helped bring the point home.

First, he had us take out an index card and list our ten greatest life successes. He didn't care if we had to go back to high school or earlier; he just wanted us to list and look at some of the things we had accomplished. My list poured out of me, and when I was finished, I read it over and over again. I was so energized!

I found that the speaker was correct: I don't think about those things enough, especially when things aren't going well. My mind then went to David when he faced Goliath. It dawned on me that David used this very principle to help him defeat the giant: "Your servant has killed both the lion and the bear; this uncircumcised Philistine will be like one of them" (1 Samuel 17:36).

How did David prepare for his battle? He drew upon the memory of his past successes. Those successes of yesterday gave him courage and faith for today. If David used that technique, why not you and me? But wait, there's more.

After we made our list of successes at the conference in Seattle, the leader directed us to make another list. This time he wanted us to list all our life recoveries that had occurred or were in the works. As I made that list, I was amazed. I was impressed by how many things I had worked through with God's help, and I was still here, productive and functioning.

I now carry both these index cards with me and look at them on a regular basis. They encourage me and serve to remind me that God has been with me, is with me, and will continue to be with me no matter what. Those two lists also remind me that I'm strong in Him and can face today and tomorrow with resolve, determination, and courage.

In a sense, you can say that I am treating these lists like a box of mints. I can't live on this list, just as I can't live on a box of mints. I can, however, choose something from that list from time to time and let it refresh me, just like a mint. I can turn it over, so to speak, in my mind and recapture the feeling of that success or recovery.

If you're like me, then you may be looking past the successes and recoveries you've already had. You're a strong person who has a track record of success or at least survival. Now it's time to learn to build upon the foundation that those successes provide.

ACTION PLAN: Get two index cards, or use your journal if you wish. Make two lists—one of your successes, the other of your recoveries. Once you're done, review what's on those lists. How do they make you feel? I hope they give you hope, joy, and peace. Don't put those lists away; keep them where you can see them every day this week. Enjoy a "success mint" when you need one this week. As you do this, know that I will be doing the same. Remember that we can face tomorrow because of God's faithfulness yesterday, today and forever.

SECTION 2

Creativity

So God created man in his own image, in the image of God he created him; male and female he created them (Genesis 1:27).

I meet many people who tell me that they are not creative. I don't believe it. In this section I will tell you why, sharing my own journey from being an administrator to a creative writer, consultant, and speaker.

My first objective in this section is to help you accept and embrace your creativity. The next objective may surprise you: to help you be comfortable with failure. Failure is an important part of the creative process for failure teaches you how to be successful, as odd as that may sound. Failure is a great teacher and every creative person has had many teachers, one of which has been failure.

Have your journal ready to record what the Lord shows you, and let's begin.

WEEK 14

Peanut Faith

George Washington Carver is one of my heroes. Carver was an African-American scientist who lived in the period following the U.S. Civil War. At a time when black Americans suffered from shameful conditions and prejudice, Carver single-handedly revolutionized agriculture in the American South. He did it through hard work and prayer.

As a professor at Tuskegee Institute in Alabama, Carver discovered that peanuts were a perfect crop for the Southern soil and climate, and he urged farmers to plant peanuts. There was only one problem: At that time there was no market for peanuts! Farmers were angry, and Carver was embarrassed. George Washington Carver prayed, however, and God gave him the solution to his problem.

The story has it that Carver began his prayer by asking, "Oh, Lord, teach me about the universe," to which the Lord responded, "That is too much for you." Then Carver prayed, "Then Lord, teach me about man."

Again the Lord responded, "You are thinking too big."

Finally, Carver cried out, "Lord, then please teach me about the peanut!" After that prayer, Carver went back to his simple laboratory, and during his illustrious career, discovered more than 300 uses for the peanut. He found ways to make fertilizer, paint, paper, and glue from peanuts. He also discovered peanut oil and peanut butter. While he was at it, he also discovered more than 100 uses for the sweet potato.

There are many lessons from Carver's life that we can apply to creativity and productivity. First, prayer is a helpful tool. If you need wisdom or insight, why not ask God for it? Second, there are many discoveries yet to be made. Why can't you be the one to discover them? Third, keep things simple. You don't need to pray about changing the *entire* world in order to serve God; you just need to pray about how to change *your* world. Armed with the knowledge of your purpose and prayer, you may discover a significant breakthrough that will touch a few or many. You may be able to take your interest in something simple and turn it into a memorable career, just like George Washington Carver did.

ACTION PLAN: Let the next seven days be days of prayer. Ask God for wisdom concerning the interests you have, no matter how small or simple they may seem to be. Then expect God to answer you, and record the answers in your journal. Be ready to learn new things this week about the seemingly small interests in your life and then yield them to God. From that, there is no limit to what God can do with and through you. Make sure you write what you see and hear as you pray.

WEEK 15
Good Ideas

Every once in a while I reflect on how amazing it is that God does His work through people. He uses us, with all our frailties and weaknesses, and seems more comfortable with our humanity than we are. I've found that many people are waiting to be more spiritual, smarter, to know more about the Bible, or to be better equipped before they attempt to fulfill their purpose. I have also found that most people are equipped to do something right now, if only they will try.

I talk to people who have an idea, but they are not sure whether that idea is a good thing or a "God" thing. Are you like that? If you are, then you may be waiting for some confirmation or sign that will enable you to know for sure and then proceed. If you're honest, you don't really trust the internal confirmation if it comes; thus you are waiting for some external confirmation.

Let's look at what Luke wrote at the beginning of his gospel. Luke was a doctor, a scientist and researcher. He wrote using the best Greek in the New Testament. After Luke researched Jesus' life and ministry, the Holy Spirit inspired him to write an account of his research. Yet look at how Luke describes his decision to write this account: "However, *it occurred to me* that it would be well to recheck all these accounts from first to last and *after thorough investigation* to pass this summary on to you, to reassure you of the truth of all you were taught" (Luke 1:3-4 TLB emphasis added).

The New Living Translation states, "Having carefully investigated all of these accounts from the beginning, *I have decided* to write a careful summary for you, to reassure you of the truth of all you were taught" (NLT emphasis added). Note what Luke didn't say in those opening verses. He didn't say, "The Lord is leading me to write." He didn't write, "It has been confirmed that it is God's will for me to write." His decision to write was just that: a decision. He said, "It occurred to me" to write. He didn't over-spiritualize the process. I've found that many people are using their desire for "confirmation" as a delay tactic. I've also found that people who say, "I'm praying about doing that" usually aren't praying; they're delaying. What has occurred to you to do? Why aren't you doing it?

God used Luke's love for investigation and research to write His Word. God also wants to use you, just as you are, to produce things for Him that are consistent with the person He created you to be. Do you have any good ideas? Stop waiting and start painting, writing, singing, building, inventing, researching, or dancing to the glory of God.

While perhaps God hasn't formally invited you to do these things, He probably hasn't told you not to do them. With that awareness, make an effort to do something that God can then take and use. I can't promise you will write a book like Luke did that will impact the world, but you may be surprised how God uses something that only seemed like just a good idea to you.

ACTION PLAN: Take your journal and turn to a fresh page. List all the excuses you can think of that could prevent you from achieving your dream. "I'm too old." "I'm too young." "I'm not educated enough." "I'm the wrong sex." Examine this list. Tear out that page from your journal and go outside with the list and a pack of matches. Burn the list. Come back inside and get working on the good ideas that you have.

WEEK 16
Better Late Than Never

If you've read this far, you know that I love London. I usually am there on ministry sometime around Christmas. On a visit a few years ago, I attended a performance of George Frideric Handel's *Messiah* at the Royal Albert Music Hall. It was a marvelous way to enjoy a timeless masterpiece of music and Scripture in the city where it was composed.

The *Messiah* is considered by many to be the greatest musical feat in history. Commissioned by a charity to be performed at a benefit concert, Handel composed it in only 24 days. A musician once told me that someone just trying to copy the *Messiah* could not do so in 24 days—that is the level of inspiration in which Handel operated. While Handel composed, he never left his house. His food trays remained untouched outside his office door. A friend who visited him as he composed found him sobbing with intense emotion. As Handel groped for words to describe what he had experienced, he paraphrased Paul, saying, "Whether I was in the body or out of my body when I wrote it I know not" (see 1 Corinthians 12:2).

What is even more impressive is that Handel wrote it under extreme duress. The Church of England strongly criticized and opposed Handel and his previous scriptural works put to music. At the age of 56, he had no money, often going out only at night to avoid his creditors. He also wrote this masterpiece while recuperating from a stroke he had suffered four years earlier.

In 1742, Handel performed his new work in Dublin— what he thought would be his farewell concert. He went home, fully expecting to end up in debtor's prison. Yet the first performance of *Messiah* raised almost 400 pounds for charity and freed 142 men from debtor's prison. Handel went on from that project to enjoy tremendous success and popularity in his latter years. The rest is history as countless millions have enjoyed and marveled at this masterpiece for more than 250 years.

What does this have to do with you? Perhaps you are a person of purpose but you're frustrated by your lack of progress or productivity. Maybe you find yourself down and out, discouraged and criticized, forgotten and a failure. Perhaps your finances are in poor shape. If any of those describe you, press on. If that's not you, press on anyway, for you will probably enter that phase one day as you pursue your purpose and attempt to be more productive.

It's important that you see this season in your life as *preparation for the next season.* No matter how old you are, you're still developing and growing. Don't allow this season of life to define you. All it takes is one phone call, letter, or meeting to change your world. Knowing that, you can continue to prepare for your success, which will certainly come later.

ACTION PLAN: Find a CD of Handel's *Messiah* and listen to some of it every day this week. Make sure that you listen to the "Hallelujah Chorus," the most famous portion of the entire work. As you listen and remember what Handel went through to write it, let your heart be encouraged and your creativity stimulated. Write your thoughts in your journal as you listen, paying special attention to the things you would like to accomplish.

WEEK 17
A Creative List of Creativity

I'm a creative person! That reality still thrills me as I learn to walk in my new sense of freedom. I hope you are experiencing the same kind of freedom as we study this section on creativity, and as you come to the realization that you, too, are creative! For me, that realization has meant that I've cast off old ways of thinking and I'm entering a new phase of productivity and purpose. As I do, I learn something new about creativity almost every day. I've even found lots of creativity in the Bible. Let me give you an example. God made Adam to be creative, and we are Adam's children. After God created Adam, He invited Adam to enter into the creative process by naming the animals:

> *Now the Lord God had formed out of the ground all the beasts of the field and all the birds of the air. He brought them to the man to see what he would name them; and whatever the man called each living creature, that was its name. So the man gave names to all the livestock, the birds of the air and all the beasts of the field* (Genesis 2:19-20).

Adam, and Adam alone, decided what the animals were to be called; it was an expression of his creative dominion in the garden.

Too often, only musicians, songwriters, poets and writers have been identified as creative. They are indeed creative, but those are only a few of the creative expressions that are available to you and me, Adam's children. Let's take a look at some of the creative expressions that are available to us in everyday life:

Child raising—Raising a child requires tremendous creativity as you teach, train, entertain, and discipline each child according to his or her personality and needs.

Handwriting—Do you have beautiful handwriting? Then stop using the computer. Use your creative, artistic flair to communicate with others in your own writing.

Dress—You may have an eye for color or fashion. Then be creative and adorn your body, God's creation, in a manner that is distinctive and uniquely you.

Repairs—It takes creativity not only to invent or design something, but to keep it in working order. Your ability to read a manual and then fix something is an expression of your creativity.

Gardening—Do you like flowers? Enjoy raising vegetables? Then plant to the glory of God and do it with your style and grace. If you don't plant the seeds, they won't grow! So join in the creative process and do what Adam and Eve did in the garden. (Don't forget to pull the weeds, too!)

Time management—Can you organize your time and activities? That requires creativity. Can you help others organize? That requires even more creativity.

Problem solving—Do you face new problems and apply timeless wisdom and solutions? Then you aren't just organized or efficient; you are creative!

I hope you get the picture. Like Adam, you are creative,

and God wants you to express your creativity in everyday life. Stop saying you aren't creative; you are!

I've posted a more comprehensive list of creative expressions that my *Monday Memo* readers helped me compile; you can read it at www.purposequest.com/misc. (look for the article entitled "Creative Expressions"). If you think of additional areas of life that require creativity, write me and I'll be glad to add them to the list. If you don't do anything else this week, however, please spend some time thinking, praying about, and identifying your specific areas of creativity. Perhaps then you'll see yourself as creative, which is just how the Lord wants you to see yourself.

ACTION PLAN: I've already alluded to what you need to do this week. Do just what I did above. Make a list in your journal of every creative expression in your life. Once you identify those areas, add a sentence or two explaining just how your creativity is expressed in those particular activities.

WEEK 18
A Creative Jesus

Jesus was a creative man. We know that He was a carpenter, so He made things from wood with His hands. One second-century bishop reported that the wooden yokes Jesus made in the first century were still being used 100 years later! That tells us that Jesus wasn't only creative; He was also committed to excellence. He did good work.

There's also a good chance that Jesus, as the oldest son, ran a carpentry business that supported more than just Himself. His brothers could have been in business with Him. That means He also expressed His creativity by running a business, making payroll, managing inventory, accounts, and customer service. He undoubtedly supported His widowed mother from the business as well.

Jesus' creativity didn't stop there. At the age of 30, He changed careers, starting an itinerant ministry through which He continued to express tremendous creativity. He was creative in building and equipping an effective team of men and women who traveled with Him. When Jesus performed miracles, He did so with flair and distinction. One time He spit on the ground, made mud and smeared it on a blind man's eyes (see John 9:6). Another time, Jesus put His fingers into a deaf man's ears and touched the end of the man's tongue with His spit (see Mark 7:33).

Jesus answered His critics with creative retorts that delighted the crowds. His insight into Scripture held people's attention for days on end with His fresh approach to God and the Word.

Perhaps Jesus' greatest creative expression, however,

was the way He taught. He used parables—stories from everyday life that imparted truth. Where did He get those stories? He made them up. They emanated from His creativity, perhaps the same creativity that He learned and perfected as a carpenter. Jesus used parables with lessons drawn from agriculture, business, current events, family life, and gardening. He was such a creative teacher that people would walk for days to hear Him, then would stay for days listening to His teaching. Mark reported, "The large crowd listened to him with delight" (Mark 12:37).

Why is this important? First of all, Jesus' creativity came from His divinity. He expressed His creativity as a Jewish man who observed life and saw God in all of it. Second, since Jesus was creative, He can help you to be creative. Finally, you'll only fulfill your purpose and be productive as you walk in your own creative expressions, just like Jesus did. We're not here on earth just to maintain; we're here to creatively advance the kingdom of God. Your creativity is the means by which you will help fulfill the mandate given to Adam to subdue the earth and rule over it.

Don't see your creativity as a quirk or something that you use only from time to time. See it as a powerful source of daily inspiration that will help you to fulfill your purpose and produce significant things. As you do, I know your life will be changed, as mine has been.

ACTION PLAN: Take some time to read Proverbs chapter 8. Do you see wisdom speaking there? That "wisdom" certainly sounds a lot like Jesus to me. Pray through this chapter of Proverbs and then ask the Lord for creative wisdom. Ask Him to help you use the ordinary lessons of daily life, just like Jesus did, to do something extraordinary. Write in your journal what you see and hear from that study.

WEEK 19

Oh Yes You Are!

At the beginning of this section, I said that when I teach about creativity, the comment I hear most frequently from people is, "I don't think I'm creative." I hope by now—week 19 of our study—that you are no longer saying that about yourself, because it simply isn't true! A creative God created you to be creative. Creativity is programmed into the very fabric of your being. You're not convinced? Then consider these expressions of creativity that are part of who you are:

• I don't want to be offensive in any way, but you were made to create other human beings. When you reach maturity and marry, in most cases you must take precautions to limit the number of children you'll have.

• Scientists tell us that every seven years you have a totally new set of cells in your body. Your cells are constantly dividing and creating new cells.

• Your body creates new hair and nails on a daily basis. That's why one of the first things I do when I return home from a long trip is to get a haircut.

• Your body is constantly creating what it needs in order to continue living. Your stomach creates gastric juices, sweat glands produce sweat, and your ears produce wax!

• What happens when you go to sleep? You create dreams; you are a "dream machine." For every eight hours you sleep, you dream almost two hours. Your mind is constantly creating symbolic sleep scenarios that help you maintain your psychological equilibrium.

• Every day you create thoughts and ideas; you also daydream, creating potential scenarios with you in them.

- You talk every day, stringing words and ideas together creatively.

Without even trying, you are truly a creative being. So why aren't you even more creative or more effective at expressing it? The big problem is in your mind. You've been conditioned to believe that you aren't creative, so it's possible to go through life convinced that you aren't. When you think you aren't creative, you won't produce or won't recognize your creativity for what it is. For many years, I saw myself as "only" an administrator who helped others get things done. Now I see myself as an administrator who creatively gets things done. That slight change of perspective has changed my life.

So if you don't do anything else this week, reassess your attitude toward your creativity.

ACTION PLAN: Revisit the list you wrote in your journal of the creative expressions in your life. Now write down some creative affirmations, such as "I am a creative person," "I solve problems with new and creative ideas," "I have an excellent sense of color when I create my jewelry, paintings or pottery," "I can easily create solutions to computer problems that perplex others," and more. I hope you get the idea. You've talked yourself out of being creative long enough. Now it's time to talk yourself into it. As you do that, it's just a matter of time before your creativity blossoms and becomes all that God intended for it to be.

WEEK 20
You're Quirky!

Do you find yourself not doing certain things because you're concerned about what other people will think? You may be worried about what your mother, father, or spouse will think, and that's certainly understandable. The approval of the people closest to us is an important thing. Often, however, it isn't even those closest to us who cause us not to step out and try something that's out of character, risky, or seemingly foolish.

Over the last few years, I've come to a startling realization in my own life about how often I haven't done something because I was concerned with how I would be perceived by others. Those "others" were people who didn't matter, sometimes people I didn't even know.

For example, I wouldn't make certain requests in restaurants because I didn't want to look foolish. I wouldn't ask for directions because I didn't want the people in the service station to think I was stupid. I wouldn't wear anything orange, my favorite color, because I was afraid that others would think it was a strange color for a grown man to wear. I think you get the idea.

Almost all people pursue behavior they consider "normal." Some people would call it being balanced. Yet normal or balanced people seldom achieve greatness or even purposeful living. They do everything that other people and society expect of them, but they stop short of doing what is in their heart to do—sometimes for fear of what others will think.

While many people pursue normalcy, I have yet to find

anyone who can describe what "normalcy" is when I ask them. What's more, none of the people I ask about normalcy are normal, including you and me. If we are going to be people of purpose, you and I must accept the fact that we are not normal.

Before you run off and say that I called you "weird," let me explain. We all have things we love that others would never understand and would perhaps even consider a bit "quirky" (which is defined as a peculiar trait). So what? To be true to yourself, you must pursue those quirks because those quirks will often lead you to your passion. Your passion is where your purpose and productivity live.

If you can play the piano all day, then play as often as possible. If you love to hike in the woods, hike. If you like the color purple, then purple your entire world. Who cares? If someone does care, it's really none of their business. I have written hundreds of *Monday Memos* and given them away, free of charge. Some people say that's not smart; others have told me it's not normal, that I'm just playing around.

Why am I encouraging you to pursue your own personal quirkiness? Why do I think this is important? It's important because you are a one-of-a-kind creation. You need to stop trying to imitate what others do and be your original self. Samuel Johnson once wrote, "No man ever yet became great by imitation." I agree. If you love chemistry, then be a chemist. If you enjoy reading, then read and read some more. If you have children and they love something, let them do it as much as possible, as long as it is not harmful to their health.

Perhaps this week you need to stop having normalcy as a goal and start having quirky as your goal. As you do, you'll be happier, and you'll have a better chance of being productive. If you continue to pursue normalcy, you'll be pursuing something that will never be achieved in your lifetime. So stop trying!

ACTION PLAN: I've met one-on-one with more than 1,500 people over the last five years to talk about purpose and productivity. Sometimes people ask me at the end of a purpose session, "So I'm not crazy?" I respond, "You are, but so is everyone else. Go be who you are!" What behavior or activity have you avoided because you were afraid others would think you strange? While you're at it, try defining what normal is. Isn't normal what's right for you, even though it may be unusual for someone else? Journal your thoughts on this matter.

WEEK 21

An Audience of One

I started writing *The Monday Memo* in 2001. Then I discovered a man named Roy Williams who writes something called *The Monday Morning Memo*. My focus is on purpose and productivity. Williams focuses on branding, ad copy, and creativity. I recommend both his Memo as well as his book, *The Wizard of Ads* (www.wizardacademy.org). They are tools to help you sharpen and focus your creativity.

In one of his Monday Morning Memos, Williams quoted Peter Drucker, the late management guru, who pointed out that business schools today are studying books that were poorly received when they were first published and didn't sell well. Williams went on to conclude that the loneliest people can often be those who create ahead of their times.

This led to a discussion of Ludwig von Beethoven, who basically gave up on his ability to please and compose for his own generation. Instead he composed for a "later age" because so many of his contemporaries criticized and ignored his work! Williams listed these quotes about people who created ahead of their time:

"When a true genius appears in this world, you may know him by this sign, that the dunces are all in confederacy against him." *—Jonathan Swift, author of Gulliver's Travels*

"Great spirits have often encountered violent opposition from mediocre minds." *—Albert Einstein*

"Funeral by funeral, science makes progress." — *Paul Samuelson*. "Yes, even scientists ahead of their times are rejected by their peers," added Williams.

Emily Dickinson wrote with complete confidence that her words would never be read. When she died, her family found 1,700 of her poems in a drawer. Many of these poems rank with the greatest ever written but were never read by anyone while Dickinson was alive. Perhaps she was being prophetic when she wrote:

Fame is a fickle food
Upon a shifting plate
Whose table once a
Guest but not
The second time is set.
Whose crumbs the crows inspect
And with ironic caw
Flap past it to the Farmer's Corn—
Men eat of it and die.[2]

Williams noted, "Dickinson wrote for herself, an audience of one. Study the lives of the Great Ones and you'll find this to be a common characteristic among them."[3]

For the last five years, I've written daily Bible studies that I send out on a weekly basis to thousands of people. I offer them free of charge. One day I hope to publish them, but if I don't, I'm still committed to do a study for every book in the New Testament. When I talk to people about my vision to publish them, everyone tells me, "Bible studies don't sell well." They will never sell if they are not published, and they will never be published if I don't write them, so I keep writing in the hope that one day they'll be published.

The application for you is simple. Do you have something new and different to say or do? Are you willing to write or perform for an audience of one? If so, then get busy this week being true to who you are and don't pay attention to what others think or say. Just do it. Better yet, just be it.

ACTION PLAN: What can you do in hope? What do you want to do that you may do only for your own sake—an audience of one? Write out your plan of what you will do and how you will feel if no one pays attention or gives you much encouragement. Once you do that, I trust you will be ready to produce for an audience of one, if need be.

WEEK 22
Draw a Picture

I mentioned in week 17 that I'm a creative person. As you know, I didn't always think that about myself. A few years ago, I changed just one word in my purpose statement, but it was a profound change. Prior to the change, my statement read that I "bring order out of chaos." Then one day it occurred to me: *I don't bring order out of chaos, nor do I make order out of chaos. Rather I create order out of chaos.* I made this one-word change after it dawned on me that I'm a creative person. That insight changed my life!

Up to that point, I had always viewed myself as an organized, administrative-type person. I saw musicians, songwriters, and poets as the creative people, while I organized their creativity and brought order to their world. Then I saw the light! I saw that my ability to "bring" order is in and of itself a creative act.

A few weeks before I saw this change, I was heading to Uganda with a team from my home city. On the plane, the team leader asked each of us to fill out a form outlining our goals and objectives for the trip. Then she asked us to do something that would normally bring fear to my heart: She asked us to draw four pictures on the back of the paper to describe ourselves before, during, and after the trip.

I actually felt my body stiffen as she asked us to draw those pictures because I can't draw, or so I thought. Right there on the plane, I decided to face my fear of being ridiculed and not being very "good," and proceeded to draw four very simple but effective pictures. They were the first pictures I had drawn in 40 years.

After I drew them, I took out a sheet of paper and listed all the areas in which I was creative. Here's how my list read: humor, consulting, conference and event coordination, writing *The Monday Memo*, my weekly Bible studies, seven books, public speaking, my daily to-do list, my web site, the seminars that I teach, and the two businesses that I've started. These are all creative acts; therefore, I am creative! I do, indeed, create order out of chaos.

If I have not already convinced you in this section that you, too, are creative, let me reiterate the point: You *are* creative. You are creative because the Creator made you in His image, and part of that image is to create. You may not see yourself as creative, but He does. (And do you want to tell Him that He's wrong?) You may not have any original ideas (who does?), but you probably have ideas of how to apply concepts that already exist in new and creative ways.

I also write this to help you overcome any bias that you may have against your creativity. Stop comparing what you create with what others create. This week let your creativity flow, just like I did with my four pictures. Your creativity may hold a key to help you clarify your purpose and be more productive.

Facing the fact that you are creative may set you free to do the things that have been in you to do all along. I'm enjoying my new awareness of my creative expression, and from now on, I'll tell everyone and anyone that my purpose is to create, not bring, order out of chaos. I hope this lesson will give you a renewed sense of who you are and what you were created to create.

ACTION PLAN: I have referred to my purpose several times, which is to create order out of chaos. What is your purpose? Go to Appendix Two where you will find a worksheet with questions and ideas to help you bring clarity to your purpose. You need this clarity, no matter what your purpose, if you are going to be as productive as possible. Use your journal to record what you believe your purpose is.

WEEK 23

Three Enemies

Last week I described a major change in my purpose statement. I no longer say that I *bring* order out of chaos; I now realize that I *create* order out of chaos. Since embracing my own creativity, I've done a lot of reading and study on creativity. That helped me to develop a creativity seminar that has helped others embrace their own creativity.

Shortly after I added the word *create* to my purpose statement, Tom Deuschle, my friend in Zimbabwe, made a statement in a business seminar that has stayed with me: "An oppressed people lose their creativity." Tom lives in a country where he knows all about oppression, and he pastors a large church in the capital city that has grown dramatically (and creatively) in the midst of horrific conditions. As I pondered Tom's statement, I thought of the Israelites in Egypt, where they were oppressed and enslaved by their taskmasters. Tom is right; they had lost their creativity. Perhaps we could more accurately say that their creativity was not lost, but rather redirected toward daily survival as they tried to eke out an existence under the oppression of slavery.

Then it occurred to me that there is another form of oppression that also saps creativity. The Jews in Egypt were under external oppression, but I've known people who are under a far worse creative limitation—they are under *internal* oppression. Their greatest barrier to creativity isn't outside themselves, but inside.

There are at least three factors that can oppress you

58

from within and keep you from being the creative person that God wants you to be:

Fear. There are many fears that could prevent you from being creative, such as fear of: failure, poverty, ridicule, family, culture, authority, rejection, inadequacy, and success. If you are going to release your creativity, you must face and overcome the oppression of fear. It paralyzes you and causes you to procrastinate. Remember what Paul wrote to his disciple Timothy: "For God has not given us a spirit of fear, but of power and of love and of a sound mind" (2 Timothy 1:7 NKJ).

Comparison. When you look at what you do and compare it to what others do, it causes you to stop being creative because, in your opinion, your creation isn't ever as good. Think about it: What is good where creativity is concerned? Isn't creativity a process? Can your simple efforts today lead to stellar creativity tomorrow? Is it wise to compare your initial efforts to what someone else may have spent a lot of time developing? Paul described an important principle that he used when he looked at his work: "We do not dare to classify or compare ourselves with some who commend themselves. When they measure themselves by themselves and compare themselves with themselves, they are not wise" (2 Corinthians 10:12-13).

Perfectionism. Next week I will introduce you to the little old man who lives inside you, waiting to criticize and disqualify whatever you create because it isn't "good enough." I know only One who is perfect and He is God. You are not (God or perfect). While you should strive for excellence and your best performance, you can never expect it to be perfect. The pursuit of perfection is unrealistic and oppressive, and amounts to a form of idolatry. It will hinder you from doing something great, just because it isn't perfect. I can't find a Bible verse that talks about perfectionism, but I can find one that speaks about excellence: "Whatever you do, work at it with all your heart, as working for the Lord, not for men" (Colossians 3:23). When you learn to distinguish between excellence and perfection, you'll be liberated to create.

Are you living under an internal, self-imposed oppression that is stifling your creativity? Which of the three oppressors are you under? When you can answer that question, your liberation is near! God wants you to be creative. This week I urge you to free yourself from any external or internal pressure that is working to hinder your creativity.

ACTION PLAN: This week's plan is simple. Remembering that fear, comparison and perfectionism are enemies of your creativity, I want you to write in your journal how those three have stifled your creativity. What can you do to defeat them? It would be wonderful if you could create something this week and share it with others. What would that creative expression be? Whatever it is, I urge you to go for it!

WEEK 24
The Cranky Old Man

If you're going to be creative and productive, you must learn to deal with the little old man who lives inside you. You may respond that you don't have a little old man living in you, but I contend that you do.

This little old man has lived in you most of your adult life. He's not only old, but also cranky. He has wrinkled skin and wears a visor on his head, similar to the one worn by old-time bookkeepers who sat under glaring lamps making calculations on ancient adding machines. This little old man has bony fingers and a scratchy voice that he uses to talk to you all the time. He doesn't have a name, but he has a role in your life that he plays to perfection. What is that role? It's the role of the critic, the censor, the discourager.

When you write something, this little old man says, "You can't write. This is no good. I wouldn't show this to anyone. You'll never get this published!" If you try to take steps to improve yourself, the man then says, "Who do you think you are? You're too old to try to do something like this!" If you have an idea for a business or ministry, he chimes in and says, "That will never work. Why don't you just stay where you are, even though you're unhappy? It's safer there."

When you are a Christian, that little old man takes on a whole new tone. "How do you know the Lord wants you to do that? Who do you think you are, Moses or Peter? There is nothing special about what you are thinking. Plus you don't have the time, money, degree, or spirituality to do it well. Just sit there and shut up. You know the mistakes you've made trying to do things in the past!"

There's no way I can describe all that this little man says to you, but I think you get the idea. If you're going to clarify your purpose and be productive, you're going to have to deal with this little old man. I've found that you cannot reason with him, for he's too persuasive and persistent for that. This critic and censor in you will urge you to dismiss an idea within five minutes of when you first receive it. He will also cause you not to talk about yourself and to hide your creativity and ideas (after all, he'll tell you, you don't want to be proud or seem super-spiritual). He'll prey on your fears and cause you to compare yourself to those who are supremely successful, causing you to cower in despair as you behold your comparative lack of talent.

So how do you deal with this little old man? Jesus said, "The kingdom of heaven has been forcefully advancing, and forceful men lay hold of it" (Matthew 11:12-13). There's no nice way to deal with this old geezer. You can't have pity on him or listen to anything he says. What do I recommend? I recommend that you poke this little old man in the eye whenever he talks to you! That's right, you must deal ruthlessly with him on every occasion that he decides to offer his two cents.

Say to him, "Thank you, but you don't know what you are talking about." And if he doesn't shut up, then you must occupy him by poking him in the eye. Just picture him holding his eye and bending over in pain. (Don't worry. He'll recover to speak again.) Then proceed to carry out the idea that you have while he is preoccupied, and you are freed from his annoying voice and worn-out accusations.

When you were young, that little old man didn't exist. You were free then to create, to be yourself, to have fun, and experiment with life. You did things just for the sake of doing them, and you learned and had fun. As you got older, however, the old man took up residence to keep you fearful, bound, and failure-free. That little old man has taken something from you, and you must take it back, with violence if necessary. He took your youthful zeal for life, and with it he took your ability to create with freedom. Now it's time to reclaim what is yours, otherwise your productivity and creativity will remain locked away with that old man holding the key.

ACTION PLAN: All right, you're not Ernest Hemingway or Vincent van Gogh. So stop trying to be. Instead, be yourself. You must do something this week that will stifle the little old man, and it must be something creative. So you decide. Maybe you can learn to ride a bike or swim. Perhaps you can draw a picture and give it to someone as a gift. Maybe you can cook or bake something and have someone over to eat it with you. Or maybe you can sketch a rough design for that invention that's been on your mind for years, and then search the internet for a local patent attorney. Wherever the critic within has put a lid on you, take the lid off this week and go for it!

WEEK 25
Your Board of Directors

This book is about releasing the power of your productivity. It isn't enough to have ideas. You must learn to bring your ideas to completion. The idea you have is only part of the creativity process; the idea isn't an end in itself. You must figure out how to go forward and express your creativity in meaningful ways. One way to do this is to establish a board of mentors, similar to a corporate board of directors, who will help you be creative.

Jesus said, "You will know the truth and the truth will set you free" (John 8:32). If you know that you are creative but have trouble expressing it, then you are free—free to team with others who can do what you can't. The answer isn't trying to be who you're not, for if you could be everything, you wouldn't need anyone else. The answer is to identify those people and even things—yes, things—that mentor you and help you produce. How can you do this?

First, don't get locked into bad thinking. You don't need a mentor; you need mentors. You need more than one. What's more, mentoring isn't a lifelong appointment. You will change mentors regularly as the needs of your creative expression change. Where can you find these mentors?" Consider the following options:

Bible characters. Who is your favorite Bible character? Why is he or she your favorite? It is probably because he or she has something that you need. Go back and study that person's life. Paul is my favorite. I read books about him and meditate about what he did. I pray to the same God who helped Paul be creative, asking Him for the same creative spirit that Paul had. Paul has directed my life and decisions, so the apostle Paul is on my board of mentors.

Historical characters. Who do you admire from the past? I admire John and Charles Wesley. I've studied their lives and how they founded Methodism. I've visited their home and cathedral in London. I've also worked with Methodists to see how the Wesleys' work continues today, 200 years after they died. Because of their work and productivity, the Wesleys are on my board of mentors.

Current leaders. Who speaks to you today? Please don't limit yourself to the church world as you consider this question. There are two men who are on my board of mentors. One is Peter Drucker, the father of modern management studies, who died just a few years ago. I read and re-read his books. The other is Robert Greenleaf, the originator of the servant-leadership message. Greenleaf died in 1991, but I financially support his foundation and read everything that his foundation produces on servant-leadership. Drucker and Greenleaf are on my board of mentors.

Associates. I have three people with whom I meet regularly who help me with my business and ministry. When I say we meet regularly, it may be once a year. We may email from time to time. I've learned to draw from their expertise in the areas of editing, finance, marketing, and business development. I also have two pastors, one in the United States and one in Zimbabwe, who speak to my spiritual needs. These five people are on my board of mentors.

Family. I draw more and more on my wife's wisdom and counsel. It is ironic that I am doing this more even though I am home less. Kathryn is a painter and designs fine jewelry, working with gold and semi-precious gems. She has an exceptional eye for color and symmetry. My son is a great photographer, and my daughter is a marketing woman extraordinaire. All of them have something to contribute when it comes to helping me express my creativity.

Now you have met my board of mentors. I mentioned above that "things" can also mentor you. For example, I try to go to Disney World regularly. The concept of an entire place devoted to creativity and excellence challenges me to do more as I study what they do and how they do it. In addition, I go to two conferences annually, both of which inspire and equip me. I also read *Fast Company* magazine from cover to cover every month.

You get the idea. You need to surround yourself with people and things that will support and affirm your creativity. If you don't, then you may find you've surrounded yourself with people who try to talk you out of your ideas rather than into them. You may already have a good board of mentors in your life, but if you don't, it's time to get some, and fast. Once you find a team who will stimulate and encourage your creativity, you will never want to be around those who hinder your creativity again.

ACTION PLAN: Are you ready to identify your board of mentors? Use the categories I've listed above and build a team to help you be more creative. What authors or artists will be among your mentors? What places can you visit that will stimulate your creativity? Who among the living or the dead will make it onto the list? Make sure you write these names in your journal and add a sentence or two about what role these people (or things) either now play, or will play, in your creative life.

WEEK 26
Write Yourself a Letter

When I admitted several years ago that I was creative, I started teaching creativity—creatively teaching it, I might add! I always enjoy hearing from people who have attended my sessions who went on to publish a book, start a business or bring some creative expression from dream to reality.

Once I started paying attention to my creativity, I began noticing what others had to say about creative efforts. Here are a few quotes for you to think about:

"A great deal of talent is lost to the world for want of a little courage. Every day sends to their graves obscure men whose timidity prevented them from making a first effort." —*Sydney Smith*

"Everyone has talent. What is rare is the courage to follow talent to the dark place where it leads." —*Erica Jong, American author*

"Not what I have, but what I do is my kingdom." —*Thomas Carlyle, Scottish essayist and historian*

"A man is the sum of his actions, of what he has done, of what he can do, nothing else." —*Andre Malraux, French novelist and archaeologist*

"You can either take action, or you can hang back and hope for a miracle. Miracles are great, but they are so unpredictable." —*Peter Drucker, Austrian-American management consultant and educator*

"Vision without action is merely a dream. Action without vision just passes the time. Vision with action can change the world." —*Joel Barker, American business writer and speaker*

Do you have a favorite quote about creativity? How about a good example of creativity from someone's life? If so, go to my blog at www.johnstanko.us. Click on the creativity heading on the right side of the page and send me what you've found so that others can read it, too.

ACTION PLAN: Each quote above addresses doing something with your creativity or talent. That's why I am ending this section the same way I end my creativity seminars. I recommend that you get a sheet of paper and write (or type) yourself a letter. Make a creative covenant or contract with yourself. In this letter, outline your creative commitments to yourself for the next six months. What will you write and how much? Will you resume, or begin, music or drawing lessons? Will you start your business? How many paintings will you finish in the next 24 weeks? What specific steps will you take to move forward on the creative dream that has been in you for decades? Be as specific as you can.

When you've finished your letter, put it in an envelope, address it to yourself, put a stamp on it and give it to a friend, associate, or family member (preferably one who is organized). Ask them to mail this letter to you in six months. When you receive it, use the letter to evaluate how well you kept your creative covenant with yourself. Whatever you do, don't let another day go by without doing something to express your creativity. By doing this, you will foster a creative cycle that will build your creative confidence.

SECTION 3

Personal Development

Do not neglect your gift, which was given you through a prophetic message when the body of elders laid their hands on you. Be diligent in these matters; give yourself wholly to them, so that everyone may see your progress. Watch your life and doctrine closely. Persevere in them, because if you do, you will save both yourself and your hearers (1 Timothy 4:14-16).

You are the instrument through which God creates. Therefore, you must do some work to fine-tune and polish that instrument.

In this section, we will take some simple steps to prepare you for success and productivity. You are worth the investment of time and money, for this investment will produce great returns. Many people are hesitant to invest in themselves because they feel it is selfish or they are concerned about what others may think.

When athletes exercise, it is an act of personal development—but is it a selfish act? If their exercise makes them a better player on the team, their exercise in self development is really part of team development. You need to see your personal development in that light, and this next section will help you to do that.

WEEK 27
Tough Decisions

I always wanted to wear out a Bible. Instead I've worn out only one page—the one with Acts 6:1-7. I've begun every purpose seminar and message I've ever given with those verses, and that page in my Bible bears the evidence. Those verses have a lot to do not only with purpose, but also with productivity. Let's look at them and also at some important points to help you in your pursuit of productivity.

In those days when the number of disciples was increasing, the Grecian Jews among them complained against the Hebraic Jews because their widows were being overlooked in the daily distribution of food. So the Twelve gathered all the disciples together and said, "It would not be right for us to neglect the ministry of the word of God in order to wait on tables. Brothers, choose seven men from among you who are known to be full of the Spirit and wisdom. We will turn this responsibility over to them and will give our attention to prayer and the ministry of the word." This proposal pleased the whole group. They chose Stephen, a man full of faith and of the Holy Spirit; also Philip, Procorus, Nicanor, Timon, Parmenas, and Nicolas from Antioch, a convert to Judaism. They presented these men to the apostles, who prayed and laid their hands on them. So the word of God spread. The number of disciples in Jerusalem increased rapidly, and a large number of priests became obedient to the faith (Acts 6:1-7).

Here are some principles that you can apply from these verses:

Face reality. As a career or business grows and develops, the owners must face reality on a regular basis and ask, "What is working and what isn't?" You need to apply that question to your own life, job, or ministry. Are there new opportunities that you can't work on because you're too busy? Is there something that was flowing smoothly a few months or years ago that isn't going as well now? Have you lost your joy and enthusiasm? A number of years ago, I had to face the reality that I wasn't happy. I didn't have any joy of the Lord in what I was doing, although I was still capably performing my duties. Facing reality can be hard, but it can also be exciting to study the clues that will lead to exciting new ventures.

Embrace change. When you get too busy or when a project has come to the end of its usefulness, then it's time to embrace, not resist, change. You may be ready for a new position or title, or you may need to face the fact that you can't do it all. You may need to give some of your responsibilities to someone else or phase out a role you've played for some time. Even in your family, you may need to embrace the changes that come as children mature and your spouse changes. You can't make any progress, however, if you're holding on to the past. I had to embrace the change and resign from my jobs to start PurposeQuest International. It has been challenging, and there were times I woke up in the night thinking, "What am I doing? I must be crazy!" But it was time to face reality and embrace change. I didn't say to *endure* change, but rather to *embrace* it!

Feed opportunities and starve problems. I'm not advocating change for change's sake. You don't want to do something different simply for the adrenaline rush it can bring. You need to be honest with yourself, however, and ask, "What is taking more energy than ever for me to do?" "What new opportunities await if I face the reality that something isn't working any more?" "What could I do if I weren't spending so much time trying to hold on to something whose end is near?" For example, I didn't develop *The Monday Memo*, my weekly email newsletter, until I first created the time by resigning two salaried positions. Now I'm writing to people all over the world. I am working on several books and have the chance to travel to help people who need my help. There were plenty of opportunities out there, but I didn't even know what they were because I was too busy solving problems instead of feeding opportunities.

ACTION PLAN: As you enter another week, I urge you to apply these three principles to your work, family, business, or personal life. Take a look at reality (both good and bad), embrace any changes that may need to occur, and start to feed your opportunities and starve your problems whenever possible. Stop wasting creative energy on maintaining the past and invest that energy in the future. Find the answers to the questions I have raised above, and then develop strategies to jettison the old and embrace the new, using your journal to help you focus. It may not be easy, but it will bring rewards that will make you more productive and fulfilled.

WEEK 28
The Funnel Effect

I have been teaching about purpose since 1991 and recently I have noticed a phenomenon among those who have clarified their purpose. I call it the "funnel effect."

To explain it, let's think about a funnel for a moment. A funnel is wide at the top and narrow at the bottom to enable the user to pour liquids into something that has a small opening. When you begin your quest for purpose, you are at the top of the funnel. The entire world and all its options are available to you.

Then something occurs that can unnerve you and make you uncomfortable. As you progress down the funnel of purpose, you begin to feel restricted in your activities. Things you once did suddenly have no meaning, or you lose your enthusiasm for activities you once had the energy to complete. You also may find that you evaluate everything you do differently. As you go down the funnel, you find there is no room or time to do some of the things that are no longer related to your purpose or goals.

If that's happening, you may be concerned that your life will be less meaningful once you get to the bottom of the funnel. You may not see how God can use you when you seem to be doing so little. To the contrary, the bottom of the funnel is your point of greatest effectiveness. It's at that point where you find what you do that no one else can do. While it seems restrictive, that point allows God to send you anywhere in the world that needs who you are and what you do. The narrow point is why the funnel exists; without it, there would be no purpose for the funnel.

Here is an example to show you what I mean. History tells us that Mozart was a virtuoso violinist and pianist. Rarely in history has anyone been a world-class performer on two instruments. Mozart was so good at both that he gave up playing the violin! Mozart knew there weren't enough hours in the day to practice, so he decided to focus on what would serve him best as a composer. That is the funnel effect in Mozart's life.

How about you? Are you uncomfortable as you travel down your purpose funnel? Does the thought of restricting your activity according to your purpose or goals scare or concern you? Don't worry. The bottom of my funnel is to create order out of chaos. Armed with that knowledge, I know what I'm supposed to do, and I've eliminated many activities that aren't related to my purpose. That kind of focus has enabled me to travel the world, confronting chaos wherever I go. If the funnel effect hasn't limited my effectiveness, it won't limit yours. Trust the process so that as you progress down the funnel, you'll enjoy wherever it takes you.

ACTION PLAN: Spend some time this week thinking about where you are as you progress down your purpose funnel. You may want to draw a funnel in your journal and pinpoint where you think you are in the funnel of life. What activities, roles or jobs do you think you may need to stop doing to be more effective? What will you have to do to stop doing those things without hurting your family, organization or co-workers? Who can you train to take your place? What will you do with the time that is freed once you stop doing certain things?

WEEK 29
Self-Talk

I must confess that at times I *fight* discouragement. Notice I said I fight discouragement, not that I *am* discouraged. Sometimes I have to work hard to stay on top of my world and affirm the things that I know to be true. I want to share how I do that with you, because I know from the mail I get that you fight discouragement, too.

When I deal with discouragement, I always think of David and the story of one of his failures in 1 Samuel chapter 30:

> *When David and his men came to Ziklag, they found it destroyed by fire and their wives and sons and daughters taken captive. So David and his men wept aloud until they had no strength left to weep. David's two wives had been captured—Ahinoam of Jezreel and Abigail, the widow of Nabal of Carmel. David was greatly distressed because the men were talking of stoning him; each one was bitter in spirit because of his sons and daughters. But David found strength in the Lord his God* (verses 3-6).

How did David find this strength? The Bible tells us *where* he found it (in the Lord his God), but it doesn't tell us *how* he found it. Did he go off alone? Probably. Did he pray? Possibly. Did David review God's past faithfulness to him? Maybe. We can only guess what David did, but the important thing is that he encouraged himself and found strength in the Lord his God.

75

So what do I do when I fight discouragement? I make faith confessions and affirmations. I say things that I know to be true, finding strength in my God as I speak. As I share my affirmations with you, I hope that you will develop your own and use them to maintain your sanity in the midst of occasionally insane circumstances. Here are some of my affirmations:

• The purpose message is a powerful tool that helps people, churches and businesses find peace, joy and prosperity.
• I'm a popular author who has something to say. My books and articles are eagerly read by people who find them helpful and useful.
• I'm a speaker who is relevant and entertaining; people lose track of time when I speak.
• I coach and mentor leaders all over the world so that they can be effective and successful.
• I don't teach yesterday's methods. I'm aware of current leadership trends and skills that make me a wise and knowledgeable consultant.
• My work provides for my needs and the needs of my family so that we have enough to meet our obligations with some left over.

Is this what David did in 1 Samuel chapter 30? I have no idea. This, however, is what John Stanko does as you read this book. I'm probably somewhere in the world closing my eyes and repeating the things that I know to be true regardless of what I see or feel. I'm picturing my ideal world, not because I can create it by the power of my own will, but because I believe that this is *my* reality in the power and will of God. By doing this, like David, I find strength in the Lord my God.

ACTION PLAN: Don't just sit there; encourage yourself! Take out your journal and write your own affirmations. Please don't say "I will" or "I hope to" or "Maybe I can." Affirm who you would like to be and what you would like to do, not in wishful terms, but in positive terms such as "I am." Don't be wishy-washy or use hopeful language. Use strong, forceful language that will uplift and encourage you. When no one is around to encourage you, then you must encourage yourself. And if you're going to encourage yourself, then do a good job of it. Work as hard encouraging yourself as you would if your spouse, children, or best friends were discouraged. Do what David did, or if you need a more recent example, do what I am doing.

WEEK 30
Permission Granted

Recently I went to Kenya where I helped coordinate a tour featuring the Celebration Choir from Zimbabwe. It certainly brought back memories of the days when I coordinated tours and organized worship seminars for Integrity Music. It was during that time that I began to travel in earnest and teach workshops about purpose and goals. I have many fond memories of that season in my life.

That season, however, is over. The entire time that I was on that recent tour in Kenya, I thought, "Did I really do this for a living at one time?" It was strange because I loved what I did when I was with Integrity Music. I admit, I enjoyed some of the aspects of the Kenyan tour, but I no longer enjoy the pressures of putting on an event that takes so much work for everything to go right (and when so much can still go wrong because there are so many things beyond one's control).

That's the point I want to make this week. You must give yourself permission to grow and for things to change if you're to be productive. When things change, and when you change, don't spend time and energy trying to recapture what is gone. When a season is over, it's over. Learn to let it go gracefully.

I once spent time with a businessman who was trying to talk himself out of how he felt. There was an aspect of his company that was making money and was something he had done for many years. In some ways, however, he was emotionally attached to that work. Yet the joy was gone, and he was wrestling with the fact that he didn't have time to build other aspects of his business because that particular division took so much of his creative energy. By the end of our three-hour session, he decided to let it go to pursue other things. I think he made the correct decision.

Has something changed in you or your work? The answer may not be to redouble your efforts to capture what is gone. The answer may be to discover new areas where you can invest your energy with renewed enthusiasm. I'm not spending any time trying to recover my long-gone love for event planning and touring. Instead I want to invest my life and energy in writing, giving seminars, and eventually having a role in the broadcast media. That's where there is life for me today.

I thank God for my past work as an event planner, but I also thank God that it is in the past. I've moved on to bigger and better things, and I'm happy. Part of your happiness may lie in moving on from where you are. If you want to be more productive, then you must embrace doing things that will stimulate your creativity and passion. If you have the courage to do that, then you will continue to grow, and your growth will lead you to new and exciting opportunities.

ACTION PLAN: It's journal time again. Is there anything that belongs in your past that you are trying to keep in the present? If there is something that needs to end, I urge you to be honest with yourself and let it go! Write down what it is and why you're afraid to let it go. Is it money? Reputation? Fear of the future? There's so much more ahead for you, but first you must decide to move ahead. I'm not saying it will be easy. It requires great courage to face reality. But if you don't, you will never find all that God has for you to do. What would help you to let go? Write that down as well.

WEEK 31
Oily Joy

I was sitting in a radio studio with my headset on, ready to promote the school where I am a board member and professor. I had gone over the questions with the show host, and we were ready to go. The red light came on, indicating that we were on the air, and the host looked at me and asked a question that he hadn't mentioned in our briefing. It was not about the school at all. "Dr. Stanko," he asked, "how would you define success based on your purpose teaching?"

I was stunned and knew I had to come up with an answer quickly. After I answered, his telephone lights erupted, and my 20-minute interview ran for 60 minutes. Unfortunately, we never got around to talking about the school. What did I say that caused such a response?

When the host asked me that question, I responded, "I would define success as doing what you love. I think success is finding work that gives you joy." Just those two simple phrases touched so many listeners that I took phone calls at my home office for two weeks after the show. Since that show, which was a while ago, I haven't changed my definition of success. In fact, I feel more strongly than ever that you should do what you enjoy as often as possible, for as long as possible, if you are serious about being productive.

Here is a verse that reminds me of that: "Therefore God, your God, has set you above your companions by anointing you with the oil of joy" (Hebrews 1:9).

The oil of joy—what a great phrase that is. Of course that verse refers to Jesus' earthly ministry. That verse didn't refer to preaching, although Jesus preached. It wasn't about teaching, although He taught. It wasn't about healing, but He certainly healed. All those magnificent activities were by-products of something called *the anointing*, and the anointing was found in the joy that Jesus felt and received when He did all those things.

Joy is the main indicator and barometer that you are in the will of God. If you feel joy when you play the piano, then play. It's that simple. If you sense joy around children, then connect with as many children as possible. If you love to sing, then sing in every venue and every opportunity you have. It's not about money, prestige, or fame. It's about the sense that you are doing what you were created to do.

What can you do this week to capture this joyful anointing? For one thing, you can be honest with yourself. You can stop fighting it and embrace it. You can say to yourself and others, "I'm happiest when I'm doing this or that." You can also stop trying to manufacture joy where you don't find it and probably won't ever find it again.

People ask me if I ever get tired of all the travel I do. I can honestly say I don't. In fact, I find it exhilarating. I get joy out of traveling. I also find that travel actually helps me to finish projects and get more work done. Whenever I prepare to leave home, I have my prioritized task list in front of me at all times, which helps me to stay on track and get things done before I leave. While traveling, I have a chance to read and study, which energizes me and brings me joy. I want you to know the joy that I feel when I travel. I'm no one special. I think God wants you to have that same joy. Stop fighting it and go with the flow—the flow of anointing that comes from doing what you love to do.

ACTION PLAN: Be honest. Where is your oil of joy? What do you do that you love? What activities cause you to forget what time it is? What can you do that will make you miss a meal? Is there anything in your life right now for which you've lost your joy? What are you prepared to do about the things that you've discovered? Make sure you record the answers in your journal.

WEEK 32
Balance Is Bunk

In the past five years, I've met one-on-one with almost 1,500 people to coach them on their personal purpose and productivity. That's almost one person every day for five years! As a result of that experience, I believe I have a unique perspective and understanding of the challenges that people face in being purposeful and productive.

One of the phrases I hear all the time is, "Yes, but." If I ask people, "Do you hate your job?" they answer, "Yes, but I can't quit."

"Are you good at what you do?" "Yes, but it's not me. It's the Lord."

"Do you want to travel?" "Yes, but I'm not sure it's God's will."

"Do you want to be in ministry full time?" "Yes, but I'm not sure if it's the right time or season."

"Are you ready to do God's will in your life no matter what the cost?" "Yes, but I want balance and don't want to go overboard on any one thing."

I've come to the conclusion that "yes, but" people are usually professional excuse-makers. They use their magnificent creativity to concoct all kinds of reasons why now is not the time for them to produce, shine, or make an impact. I've also concluded that "yes, but" is really the same answer as "no." It's just that "yes, but" sounds a whole lot better.

Let's look more closely at that last excuse: the desire for balance. Many people stop short of effectiveness because they don't want to go overboard. They want to be balanced. They want to have faith, but not excessive faith. They want to address racism, but not make anyone unhappy or uncomfortable. They want to see world-class results in their life, but not have to pay a world-class price.

I challenge you to name one person who made a difference in the world who was balanced. Was Martin Luther or Martin Luther King? How about Nelson Mandela or Florence Nightingale? Perhaps Winston Churchill or Billy Graham?

You may respond that those were great people who had a unique purpose to fulfill. All right, then think of your favorite teacher when you were growing up. Were they balanced, or were they passionate about teaching and learning? Think of your favorite athlete or singer. How did they achieve that special place in your mind? They did it because they were totally committed to their craft, or their purpose. I doubt that they were "yes, but" people, but rather "yes-and-here's-how-we-will-do-it" people.

I believe that balance is bunk—a myth that we pursue in our minds. The pursuit of balance makes us unproductive and, at times, boring. Listen to yourself this week and see if you're in the habit of saying, "Yes, but." If you are, then keep the *yes* and get rid of the *but*. From there, I urge you to get busy giving the world what you have that it needs.

ACTION PLAN: Where have you said, "Yes, but"? Why do you do that? What makes you hesitant to go forward to be productive? Your assignment this week is to research one of the people I mentioned above. Find a summary of that person's life and spend 15 minutes reading about it. Where would the world be without his contribution? What if that person had said, "Yes, but..."? Now what can you do to get busy so that the world can enjoy what *you* have to offer?

WEEK 33
Bluegrass Special

I recently watched a concert on public television featuring a band from St. Louis, Missouri, called Rhonda Vincent and the Rage. I had never heard of Rhonda or her group, but her voice caught my attention. Rhonda and The Rage are a bluegrass music group. (For those outside the U.S., bluegrass is a particular style of country-and-western music.)

The Rage featured a violin, viola, mandolin, cello, upright bass fiddle, banjo, guitar, and Rhonda's fantastic voice. When I went to her website at www.nemr.net/~rhondav, I learned that Rhonda has been voted outstanding female singer by the International Bluegrass Music Association for the past seven years. I liked some of her songs so much that I downloaded them to play on my iPod.

"So what?" you may be asking. "John Stanko is into bluegrass music now. Big deal." No, I'm not into bluegrass music, but I sure got into reading about Rhonda Vincent. You know what I found out? Rhonda Vincent isn't balanced! In my opinion, that's the key to her phenomenal success in the world of bluegrass music.

Rhonda had 22 concerts scheduled in the next two months. After that, she was taking a month off, and then had 19 more concerts booked for the following two months. I think 41 concerts in five months is a lot of concerts, don't you?

Rhonda writes music and does a lot of recording, too. She is totally committed to her love, her passion. That is who she is, and she has impacted her sphere of influence like no other woman has ever done. I doubt if the word balance is in her vocabulary.

If that's what one woman can do in her field, what can you do? You won't do much if you choose to pursue balance. Balance is boring; passion changes lives. Balance causes you to be mediocre at doing a few things; passion drives you to be the best at one thing. You may say, "I can do my best when I do a little work, then a little family time, and then a little ministry time." I say, "Focus on one at a time and devote yourself to being the best that you can be, whether it's being a parent, worker, or pastor.

Was the apostle Paul balanced? Were Peter, James and John? How about Ernest Hemingway, Mother Teresa, or Beethoven? We know who those people are because they were passionate; they pursued what they did best with abandon.

The world is in desperate need of who you are and what you can do. Please don't hide behind the balance myth; let your flame burn brightly and intensely for as many as possible to see. As you do, you'll take your place with the Rhonda Vincents of the world who have decided to make their mark by being the best they can possibly be in their chosen vocation.

ACTION PLAN: Take out your journal. Choose three people who come to mind, whether living or dead, who were or are successful in their chosen field. How did they get successful? What price did they have to pay? Were they controversial? What could they have done better? Why did you choose them to analyze them? What lessons do they hold for you? What can you learn from their mistakes? Record your thoughts on the issue of balance we looked at this week. Do you agree or disagree with what I've written? Why or why not?

WEEK 34
Failure Is a Good Thing?

Nobody enjoys failure. It can bring pain, suffering, and embarrassment. Some people never get over the effects of a failure, spending the rest of their lives in regret and anguish. Yet failure along with a proper attitude and response to it are crucial if we are going to be productive. That's right: Failure is an important part of success.

Newsweek magazine published an article called "Failure Is the Best Medicine." The opening paragraph read:

> The [2001] dot-com collapse may have been a disaster for Wall Street, but here in Silicon Valley, it was a blessing. It was the welcome end to an abnormal condition that very nearly destroyed the area in an overabundance of success. You see, the secret to the valley's astounding multiple-decade boom is failure. Failure is what fuels and renews this place. Failure is the foundation for innovation.[4]

Failure is the foundation for innovation. What a remarkable statement! When you think about it, you often learn more from your failures than your successes. Failure causes you to ask, "What went wrong?" so that you can do a better job the next time. Failure shows you what didn't work and why, and sets the stage (if you don't give up) for eventual success.

If that's true, then why are you so afraid of failing? If failure is the foundation for innovation, why haven't you recovered from your last failure? If you want to be a person of purpose and productivity, you must learn to understand the role that failure has in your life and personal development.

Of all people, Christians should have a unique view of failure, for they are people of the Bible. The Bible has many stories about failure. Moses struck the rock; David had an affair with Bathsheba; Israel turned its back on God; Peter denied Jesus; Saul persecuted the early church.

Yet each of those personal failures was the basis for innovation, change, and success. Moses gave way to Joshua, who led the people of God to the Promised Land; David and Bathsheba gave birth to Solomon, a great king; Peter was one of the founders of the early church; and Saul became Paul, the great leader of the Gentile church.

Many people quote the words found in Romans 8:28, but quoting isn't always doing. The verse states: "And we know that God causes all things to work together for good to those who love God, to those who are called according to His purpose" (NAS). Armed with this important truth, why are you still agonizing over your past failures? If this verse is true, why are you so paralyzed at the possibility of making a future mistake? Learn what you can from the past failures you've had and move on. Then be prepared for your future failures that will help teach and mold you into the person you are striving to be.

The *Newsweek* article ends by stating:

> The dot-comers are already hatching new companies. Many are revisiting good ideas executed badly in the '90s, while others are striking out into entirely new spaces. This happy chaos is certain to mature into a new order likely to upset a tottering establishment, as it delivers life-changing wonders to the rest of us. But this is just the start, for revolutions beget

revolutions. So let's hope for more of Silicon Valley's successful failures.

ACTION PLAN: Wouldn't this week be a good one in which to "hatch" new things? Isn't it time that you busy yourself with your next "successful failure"? Use the week ahead to deal with your attitude toward failure. Allow the truth of Romans 8:28 to go deep down inside you, then move on and take steps toward achieving your dream. Perhaps it would help if you made a list in your journal of all the things that you are afraid of—failure, ridicule, poverty, bankruptcy, your mother, or your supervisor. Once you face those fears, what can you do this week to overcome them so that you can be more productive?

WEEK 35
Never Too Young, Never Too Old

Much of the mail I receive is from people who are discouraged. They are distressed about finances, their jobs (which they usually hate), not knowing their purpose, or past failures.

If you are discouraged and ready to give up, or know someone who is, perhaps these stories will motivate you. R.H. Macy failed seven times before his famous department store in New York became a success. English novelist John Creasey received 753 rejection slips before he published 564 books. American baseball legend Babe Ruth struck out 1,330 times, but he also hit 714 home runs.

Think you're too old? Pope John XXIII became pope at the age of seventy-six. Golda Meir became prime minister of Israel at seventy-one. George Bernard Shaw had a play produced when he was eighty-four.

Think you're too young? William Pitt II was 24 when he became prime minister of Great Britain. Mozart was just seven when his first composition was published. American founding father Benjamin Franklin was a newspaper columnist when he was 16, and then helped frame the United States Constitution when he was eighty-one.

What am I trying to say? I'm saying don't give up or stop pursuing your dreams, no matter how young or old, no matter how many times you've failed, regardless of what obstacles you face. You don't know how close you may be to a breakthrough, no matter how disheartened you are today.

You also may not realize when a friend, colleague, or even someone you sit next to on the bus is discouraged. If you know some failure-to-success stories, you can use them to encourage the discouraged.

Before David became king of Israel, he went through several decades of tough times when it appeared that he would not survive, let alone become king. What did David do? We studied his response a few weeks ago: "David was greatly distressed, for the people spoke of stoning him, because the soul of all the people was grieved, every man for his sons and his daughters. But *David strengthened himself in the Lord his God*" (1 Samuel 30:6 emphasis added).

It's critical that you do something this week to strengthen yourself or someone else. If no one comes forward to help you do that this week, go looking for them. Whatever you do, however, don't spend another day languishing in the abyss of despair. Don't let anyone you know stay there either.

ACTION PLAN: Take some time to think about the people in your sphere of influence. Choose seven people to encourage, one every day for the next seven days. Speak some kind words, write an encouraging note, buy a small gift, or do whatever else you can do to encourage those around you. Don't wait to receive encouragement; give it. Then reflect on the life of someone mentioned above who knew failure before they knew success. What lessons can you apply to your own life that would encourage your faith and productivity?

WEEK 36
Celebrate a Failure

When I first went to Zimbabwe in 1995, I planned to be there for only one day—or so I thought. I was just passing through from South Africa on my way to London. Right before my departure, however, I visited a market where my briefcase was promptly stolen! It was Friday afternoon, and try as we might, there was no way to replace my passport (which was in that briefcase) until the following week.

To make matters worse, I was on my way to London to meet my 17-year-old son. Kathryn and I had given him a trip to Europe for his high school graduation, and we had a wonderful itinerary planned. I had to call him just hours before he was to depart and tell him that the trip was off because I was stuck in Zimbabwe until I got a new passport.

To say I was disappointed is putting it mildly. I was devastated. I ended up staying in Zimbabwe three more days before I was able to replace my stolen passport. During that time, I was constantly reminded of an important truth in a verse of Scripture, which we looked at two weeks ago: "And we know that in all things God works for the good of those who love him, who have been called according to his purpose" (Romans 8:28). I like this particular translation, for it doesn't say "all things work together for good." Rather it says, "God works for good in all things." To me, there is a big difference between those two interpretations. Do you agree?

God certainly worked some good from the loss of my briefcase. During the unexpected three days that I spent in Zimbabwe waiting for a new passport, I met people and a ministry that have become part of my life. I've since returned to Zimbabwe on numerous occasions, and the people there are now like family to me. What I thought was only a 24-hour visit has turned into a love affair with a nation and its people. From Zimbabwe, I've had many more doors of effective service open to me throughout Africa. (By the way, one year later I was able to take our son on an all-expense-paid trip to Israel and the Greek isles, and recently we spent four weeks together in Zimbabwe and elsewhere in Africa!)

There were other times of failure in my life, and when they occurred I certainly found nothing to celebrate. Perhaps my greatest failure was a business that I attempted to launch in 1981. It was a painful experience that forced me to work a second job to pay off the debt when the business failed. When I tried to make sense of that blunder, I discovered my life purpose.

Ten years later, I began to teach about purpose, drawing heavily on that failed business venture as I taught. Since then, I have shared the story of that business failure more than 1,000 times with tens of thousands of people. My business failure didn't keep me from success; it was my gateway to success. I can celebrate that failure because I know it was my tutor that led me to a unique understanding of purpose.

When failure first occurs, the pain and confusion make it almost impossible to celebrate that failure with any kind of joy or enthusiasm. At first, you must do that in faith. Eventually, however, when the wounds heal and you can be more objective, you will not only see failure for the friend that it is, but you will also be able to share the lessons you have learned with others.

Let's end with one more quote, from Thomas Edison: "Failure is not the worst thing in the world; the very worst is not to try." Did you try something that didn't quite work out? Don't hide it in the basement of your mind. Bring it out into the open and celebrate your failure for the great learning tool that it is. Then build on what you learned from that failure and try again. You'll be glad you did.

ACTION PLAN: Get ready to celebrate failure next week. You can prepare by reflecting on the role that your failures have played to make you the person you are today. Don't sweep failure under the rug any longer, but learn to celebrate the good things that come when bad things happen. You may want to collect some failure quotes or stories. There's more on how to celebrate in the next lesson.

WEEK 37
Celebrate Your Own Failure

I urge my *Monday Memo* readers to set aside a week to talk about failure. We call it Celebrate-a-Failure Week. You don't have to wait for me to declare it, however. Why not celebrate this week?

I want to be clear that the purpose of this celebration is really to encourage success. I know that sounds like an oxymoron, but it's true. One way to succeed and do the will of God is to face your fear of failure. What could you do if you weren't afraid of failing? What could you do if you didn't accept your failures as the final word? If you don't give up, there's no telling what you can do in church, school, business, or government.

Another goal is to get you to forget the past, even laugh at it, if your past includes some failure—which everyone's does. If you failed, it's time to move on. Forgive yourself, forgive the others involved, and try again. In American baseball, a batter has three opportunities to hit the ball; each missed opportunity is called a strike. After three strikes, he is out. I know people who struck out, so to speak, and took off their uniform to sit in the grandstands, content to watch others perform.

It's time that you get back in the game. If you strike out or miss the kick, don't stop trying. Failure isn't the end, unless you allow it to be. I urge you to look failure in the face and see that it is powerless to control you unless you cooperate with its intimidating ways. Failure cannot define you or your life unless you allow it to do so. By celebrating, you will make sure that failure will never have the last word as you move on to new heights of purpose and productivity.

ACTION PLAN: Here are some suggestions for how to celebrate failure this week:

If you are a pastor, talk about failure and its role in the life of the believer. Make sure you are clear that it is spiritual to fail, and be sure to include personal examples of your own failures and what you learned from them

Spend some time talking with your family, and especially your children, about failure. You may want to focus on one particular failure in your own life and what you learned from it. This will free your children from the false sense that failure is to be avoided at all costs. Maybe you can have a family failure party! Make sure you laugh a lot, even at yourself.

If you are in a small group setting, spend some time talking about your failures, how you view failure and how your fear of failure may be affecting you now.

WEEK 38

The Worst Conference in History

When I worked on staff at Integrity Music, I helped plan and organize the worst conference in the history of the world! We scheduled an event in Dallas, Texas, and we expected the conference to be well-attended and planned accordingly. At first, registrations came in slowly, but we didn't think there was anything to worry about. Then we learned right before the conference was to begin that the postal service had lost our brochures—all 50,000 of them. Only a handful of brochures were delivered. Suddenly we understood the low response.

Instead of canceling the event, however, we pulled out all the stops to spread the word that we were coming, confident we could still have a successful event. Were we ever mistaken! On the first night of the event, less than 1,000 people showed up—at a church that seated 5,000. Right after we started the event, the sound system failed. I headed for the audio booth to try to fix the problem, and when I came out, I saw worship leader Ron Kenoly on stage playing the guitar and trying to lead worship. (Ron is a fantastic singer, but he isn't known for his guitar-playing skills, believe me.) When he asked for the words to come up on the screen, we realized the projection system had malfunctioned. The bulb burned out, and the church didn't have a spare. I ran backstage to print some sheets with the song lyrics, only to discover that the copy machine was broken.

When it was time for me to take the offering, I apologized, saying that I felt like I should be paying anyone who happened to be there that evening. The event went on to lose about $15,000. I learned that weekend that a bad event is like flushing a toilet. Once you flush, there isn't any way you can stop the process; you just have to let it run its course. That is how a poorly conceived event can be.

I had two choices after that disastrous weekend. The first was to quit, which I briefly considered. The second was to take three months between Dallas and our next scheduled event and study what went wrong. I chose the latter, and we went through everything we did. We came up with a number of innovations and built in more than a few safeguards to make sure what happened in Dallas would never happen again.

By God's grace, our next event was a fantastic success. We introduced some changes that generated quite a bit of revenue, and our team was better prepared and focused. Today I thank God for that terrible Dallas event and some others that followed. I learned more from those failures than I ever did from the good events.

I also learned that a bad event isn't the end of the world. When a baseball player strikes out or a soccer player misses a wide-open goal, they don't go off the field and sit in the stands. They keep playing through their failure. In practice, they work on their technique, but in the game they keep swinging and kicking. That's what you and I need to do as well.

Don't let your failures discourage you. Don't give up on your dream. Accept that failure is a part of every successful person's life, even your own. Adjust your expectations, but don't quit! Today I can organize great events because I organized some poor ones. I didn't let my failures define me; I only permitted them to teach me. Allow your failures to do the same.

ACTION PLAN: Pick a failure from your own life and study it this week. If you don't have any or they're too painful to study, then choose a failure from someone else's life—someone like Winston Churchill, George Washington Carver, or Abraham Lincoln. What can you learn from their failures? What is there yet to learn? How has your failure affected your productivity for good or bad? Write your reflections in your journal.

WEEK 39
What Are You Afraid Of?

Seth Godin is one of my favorite business authors. I've read a number of his books, including *The Big Moo*, *The Purple Cow*, *Unleashing the Ideavirus*, and *Permission Marketing*. Godin always makes me think and has helped shape my business and career over the last ten years.

In his latest book, *Small Is the New Big*, Godin wrote about failure and fear. He makes an important distinction between fear of failure and fear of criticism. See if you agree:

> Fear of failure is actually overrated as an excuse. Why? Because if you work for someone, then more often than not the actual cost of the failure is absorbed by the organization, not you. If your product launch fails, they're not going to fire you. The company will make a bit less money and will move on.
>
> What people are afraid of isn't failure. It's blame. Criticism.
>
> We don't choose to be remarkable because we're worried about criticism. We hesitate to create innovative movies, launch new human-resource initiatives, design a menu that makes diners take notice, or give an audacious sermon because we're worried, deep down, that someone will hate it and call us on it.

"That's the stupidest thing I've ever heard! What a waste of money. Who's responsible for this?"...

Fear of criticism is a powerful deterrent because the criticism doesn't actually have to occur for the fear to set in. Watch a few people get criticized for being innovative and it's pretty easy to persuade yourself that the very same thing will happen to you if you're not careful...

So the challenge, as you contemplate your next opportunity to be boring or remarkable, is to answer these questions:

If I am criticized for this, will I suffer any measurable loss? Will I lose my job, get hit upside the head with a softball bat, or lose important friendships? If the only side effect of the criticism is that you will feel bad about the criticism, then you have to compare that bad feeling with the benefits you'll get from actually doing something worth doing. Being remarkable is exciting, fun, profitable, and great for your career. Feeling bad wears off.[5]

Are you ready to be remarkable, or are you ready to do nothing and avoid criticism? The choice is yours. As for me, I want to do something special, so bring on the critics!

ACTION PLAN: Are you afraid of failure, criticism, or both? Godin has already given you your assignment for this week. Think about something you'd like to do but are hesitant to start. Read the last paragraph in the quote above. Are you afraid of criticism? Is protecting yourself from criticism a worthy excuse to not do what is in your heart to do? If not, then what can you do to get started? Record your thoughts in your journal.

SECTION 4

Time Management

"Time management is not the ability to squeeze more hours into the day. It is not the capacity to triple-book oneself in an effort to get more things done. It's not about getting more things done at all. It's about accomplishing the important." —*Stephen R. Covey*[6]

You have the gift of 24 hours every day. It's what you do with that 24 hours that will make the difference between mere existence and productivity. You may not manage time well, not because you can't, but because you've never been trained to do so.

In this section, I share with you some of my secrets that have enabled me to master my time and be productive. I've often said that productivity isn't part of the heavenly Jerusalem; it doesn't descend from on high. Rather it's the result of hard work and hard choices of what to do and what not to do.

This section will help you know how to make those hard choices that will pay great returns in the long run.

WEEK 40
Get Real!

It seemed like a near-perfect community. The houses all looked the same and were neatly manicured and landscaped. I didn't see one thing out of place. There was a church, miscellaneous stores, a post office, and a bank. As I drove through Celebration, Florida, just outside the main entrance to Disney World in Orlando, I was impressed by the city that Disney's "imagineers" had built. My most lasting impression, however, was that Celebration, Florida, wasn't really a place to live, but rather a place to visit, a tourist attraction. If you live in Celebration, Florida, you don't live in reality. Those who live there might disagree, but that was my impression as we visited.

I don't live in reality very often, and if you're honest, you probably don't either. Judging by the mail I get and by my own planner, you and I try to do too much. We have families and jobs where we have limited control over our time. We live in an imperfect world where accidents happen, things end up taking longer than we anticipated, children need to be held, tires go flat, and the needs of others take up time—time we didn't anticipate giving and often don't have.

Yet we keep right on planning, planning as if we had total control over our time and events. The truth is, we do have some control over these events. If the full truth be told, however, we don't have control over as many as we would like.

So what does this mean for you and me? It means that we need to live in reality, not in Celebration, Florida, or any other make-believe world. You and I need to identify our values and then, with the time we have left, try to do what is most important to us. (We'll discuss values more in a future week.) My to-do list for one recent week included five projects, but I couldn't get to them, not because they weren't important, but because that week I did things that were more important. I feel good as I think about that week, not because I did everything I wanted to do, but because I did everything that was important for me to do. During that week, I maintained my priorities. That's all you and I can be expected to do.

So as you begin another week, be realistic. You aren't going to sit down and write your entire book, but can you write one chapter? You're not going to have one hour for meditation and prayer every day, but can you take 15 minutes? If you choose to spend the day with your parents, spouse, or child, that is one less day you will have to invest in something else. If, however, those things are your highest priorities based on what is most important to you, and you do them, you will have had a great week.

ACTION PLAN: What three things this week will you do with the discretionary time over which you have some control? Write them in your journal now. And when you do them, refuse to feel guilty or pressured by what you aren't doing. Use your time-management system to make sure you stay on track.

WEEK 41

You Have All the Time in the World

The father of modern management studies, Peter Drucker, said that if you have more than five goals, you actually have none since you aren't focused. If you are going to add a goal to your list of five, he said, you must decide which of the original five to eliminate.

I'm usually an optimistic person. I'm confident that I will get the things done I need to do. Consequently, I'm almost always overextended. I take on more than I should. I don't just have five main goals; I have five main goals in each of five main areas of life! That isn't just foolish; it's counterproductive.

You, too, may find it difficult to identify your top five goals. When you do, it means that you must prioritize the activities that are most important to you. That often means that something is going to have to wait. Why? Because you don't have all the time you need, but you do have all the time there is.

Do you know people you admire who are able to get many things accomplished? Have you ever thought, *I wish I was like them. I wish I had more time.* There is no magic to their ability to get things done. In fact, you have just as much time as they do—24 hours every day. It is what you do with your time that distinguishes you from them. Perhaps they focus on those things that are most important. You may be focusing on those things that are most urgent. There is a difference.

Time is the great equalizer. You may not have as much money or talent as the next person has, but you do have just as much time. Time is the great equalizer, but it is how you use your time that will set you apart as a productive person or one who wishes you were productive.

So think again when you say, "I don't have time to do that." You have the time, but you may need to stop doing something else that is less important so that you can do that new thing. Do you have the courage to stop doing something in order to do something new? If so, then you will be known as one who manages and utilizes time well.

ACTION PLAN: In your journal, make a list of all your major life roles and activities. How many are there? Is the list realistic? Rather than trying to fit it all in, why not identify activities that you need to delegate or discontinue all together? Then when you have your final list, make an effort to prioritize the activities before you. Which ones are most important? When you identify them, focus on them until they are done or until something else comes along that is more important to replace them. Enter those activities on the appropriate day in your time-management system.

WEEK 42

A Little at a Time

To achieve greatness: start where you are, use what you have, do what you can. —*Arthur Ashe, tennis player*

Do what you can, with what you have, where you are. —*Theodore Roosevelt, U.S. president*

Do not let what you cannot do interfere with what you can do. —*John Wooden, basketball coach*

I've often found that I won't do the little I can do because it isn't everything that I would like to do. For example, I won't give even a little money because I really want to give much more; I won't write my book because I don't know who is going to publish it; or I won't visit and encourage just one person because I feel I should be doing more than impact just one life. The quotes for this week all say the same thing: Do something today even though it may seem to be only a fraction of what needs to be done. Start with what you have, where you are, even though it seems to be insignificant.

For instance, I wrote my book, *A Daily Dose of Proverbs*, by devoting 20 minutes a day over a 15-month period. Since that's all the time I had to devote to that book project, I did something every day even though it was often only one page at a time. One step at a time, I reached my destination and goal. What can you do today or this week that will help you accomplish some long-term goal?

You don't have the time to learn Spanish, but can you learn one word every day this week? You may not have the money to go on a missions trip or vacation, but can you put something aside today and every day this week, even if it's only a few cents? Your business may be small, but can you make one sale today or make one call that may lead to some future business?

ACTION PLAN: First, identify one long-term goal that has been languishing in your mind and heart. Write it in your journal. Then write out an action plan of what you need to do to achieve that goal. Not sure of some of the steps? Take a guess! Then write down one thing that you can do every day this week toward accomplishing that goal. Transfer those activities to your time-management system, entering each activity on the day you think you may be able to do it. Finally, I would suggest that you tell someone on your board of mentors what you plan to do. Then repeat the same procedure next week.

WEEK 43
A Few Minutes Every Day

Why aren't you more productive than you are now? If you're like some people, you may say that you don't have enough time to write, create, study, learn, or develop new skills that will enable you to advance and grow. The truth, however, is that you have all the time in the world—24 hours every day. There is no more time available to you. Perhaps what you really meant to say is that you don't have large chunks of time to do what you would like to do.

In *The Sound of Paper: Starting From Scratch*, author Julia Cameron has this to say about the issues of time and productivity:

> Most of us think, "If only I had more time, then I would work." We have a fantasy that there is such a thing as good creative time, an idyll of endless, seamless time unfolding invitingly for us to frolic in creatively. No such bolts of limitless time exist for most of us. Our days are chopped into segments, and if we are to be creative, we must learn to use the limited time that we have.
>
> When ego is siphoned off creativity, when creativity becomes one more thing we do, like the laundry, then it takes far less time to do it. Much of our desire for creative time has to do with our trying to coax ourselves into being in the right mood to create. We want to "feel like it," and when we don't or don't quickly, we think the solution is more time. Actually,

the solution is less attention to the vagaries of mood. In short, creativity needs to become daily, doable, and nonnegotiable, something as quotidian [everyday, commonplace, ordinary] as breathing. When we make a special occasion out of our art, we rob ourselves of the time we actually have.[7]

As I stated earlier in this book, often I don't start doing something because I don't think I have enough time to finish it. When that's the case, I need more faith that God will help me use the time I do have. At other times, I don't start something because I am afraid I don't have enough time to do it *well*. When that happens, I need more courage, not more time. Why aren't you doing more? Are you afraid you don't have enough time to finish it, or you don't have enough time to do it well?

I begin every morning by writing that day's installment for my weekly Bible study. Every day I use 20-30 minutes to create something that I want to do and that God has placed on my heart to do. I have promised 6,000 people that they will get a study every week, so I must discipline myself to sit down and write. I don't even edit what I write. Investing 30 minutes a day proves to be a blessing to many people around the world.

Stop waiting for large chunks of time that will never come. Instead, seize the moments you do have and watch them add up over time. You'll then find yourself not only talking about what you will do, but actually doing it!

ACTION PLAN: What aren't you doing because you don't think you have enough time? I want you to think of one thing you have said you will do and spend 20 minutes (less than two percent of your day) doing it every day this week. It may be exercise, learning a new language, writing in your journal or answering your emails. Just 20 minutes a day will add up to 140 minutes this week, which is more than two hours. If you do that every day this month, that will add up to more than nine hours! Seize those few moments you have and see if they don't add up to be significant.

WEEK 44
Faith for Time

I spend five months a year in Africa and travel frequently in the United States when I'm not overseas. That means there are many things I have to get done before I leave home, especially if I am leaving the country. So I have a ritual that I follow before I depart, and it has helped me to be productive, not only at home, but also when I am on the road.

One week before I depart, I usually sit down for about 30 minutes and write out everything I need to accomplish before I go. Then I prioritize those activities and assign them to a certain day in the coming week when I think I can get them done. For those projects that require more time, I schedule them on multiple days. Then it becomes critical that I follow my priorities for the week as I walk out my daily plans. When there isn't enough time, I try to have faith that God will make a way for me to do what needs to get done. I trust that what I didn't get done just wasn't that important.

Joshua was faced with a similar dilemma, as reported in the book of the Bible that bears his name. At one point, Joshua had so many enemies to fight that he asked God to stop the sun. Now that's faith! God heard his prayer and the sun didn't go down for an entire day (see Joshua 10:12-15). The lesson of that story is that you and I can and need to have faith for time.

In 2 Peter 3:8, Peter wrote: "Do not forget this one thing, dear friends. With the Lord a day is like a thousand years, and a thousand years are like a day." When I read that verse one day, I asked myself, "If a day is like a thousand years with the Lord, what would an hour be like?" So I divided it all out and discovered that an hour would be the equivalent of 46 years. Then I took it one step further. I divided everything again to see what the equivalent of a minute would be. I found that one minute would be like almost nine months!

So what does that mean? If the Lord ever says He will be there in a minute, it can take a lot longer than we thought. The reverse, however, is also true. A thousand years can be like a day. What we thought could take nine months may take a much shorter amount of time to get done.

Have you been putting off things because you don't have the time? Instead of putting them off, why not put a plan together for this week that includes faith for time? Ask God to have your "sun stand still," and see if you can't get more done than you thought possible. Don't start this week with the mentality that there is no way you can get it done, but start the week with a commitment to do what you can and see if God doesn't help you do more with less. Don't be defeated before you even start. I invite you to join me in believing for a miracle this week, not only for my to-do list, but also for yours.

ACTION PLAN: Did you ever notice how much you can get done right before you go on a vacation or business trip? Why not try to replicate the dynamic that makes that possible? I recommend that you develop a list of things you would like to do in the next seven days. Then assign those tasks to one day this week in your time-management system. If you have too many things to do, keep your master list in front of you and, when some unexpected time becomes available, study that list to see what you can do. Next week, evaluate whether this worked for you, and if it did, consider doing it again.

WEEK 45

Overchoice

The key is not to prioritize what's on your schedule, but to schedule your priorities. —*Stephen R. Covey*

I sat at my desk, not doing anything except playing solitaire on my computer. It wasn't as if I had nothing to do. I had a lot of things to do. I had so much to do that I didn't know where to start, so I didn't even try. I just wasted precious time. Has that ever happened to you? Roy Williams calls it "overchoice."

We are beat up, tired, and exhausted, but it's not the things we're doing that are wearing us out. It's the burden of all the things we're not doing. It's the knowledge of things undone that causes us to wish for more hours in a day. When watching television, it's all the shows we aren't watching that drive us crazy. We have too many possibilities, too little time. Overchoice strikes again.

Overchoice is not only keeping us average, it's making us tired. We delude ourselves with the hope we can "find time" or "make time" for all the things we'd like to do, yet time can be neither found nor made. Time will continue to sweep past us at its own pace, oblivious to our existence, just as it has since the days of Adam. We cannot manage time; we can only manage ourselves. We will quit feeling tired only when we've learned to say no to overchoice.[8]

Do you feel guilty about all the things you should be doing, but aren't? Are you like me, at times wasting time because you can't decide what to do next? Or do you give your time to simpler things that you can do quickly, while neglecting those things that are most important?

Be realistic as you approach this week and every week. Perhaps you are putting too much pressure on yourself over all the things you are not doing. Can you look at the coming week and put a few things in place that will allow the next seven days to be enjoyable rather than filled with regret over lost time and opportunities? I think you can. What's more, I think you must.

ACTION PLAN: Take out your planner or calendar, and focus on the next seven days. I want you to schedule some things this week that you would like to do, things like taking your children to the park, visiting and simply talking with an elderly friend or family member, reading your favorite magazine, or doing nothing. That's right. How about putting a big "X" through one day this week and setting it aside to rest. Now there's a novel idea! Can't do a whole day? Then settle for a nap—and don't forget to schedule that nap or else you'll forget!

WEEK 46
Rest Is Hard Work

Traffic was lined up as far as I could see, but I didn't care. I was inching along on the road to the Lincoln Tunnel as I made my way into New York City. I visit New York often, and each time I do, I try to see a Broadway show or take in a sports event. When I do that, I find myself energized and refreshed in the midst of what is usually a hectic business and ministry schedule.

Now you may ask, "Why would you do that when you're already busy? Why add more to your schedule?" The only answer I can give is that a "break" like that works for me. There are times when I plan to do nothing, but coming to New York City is not one of those times. It works for me. The question I would ask is, "What works for you?"

I don't know about you, but I have to work at scheduling rest, leisure, and recreation. If I'm not careful, the rigors and demands of what I do will deplete my creativity and energy. I've got to make an effort to replenish what I lose. I imagine that the same is true for you.

What energizes you? Is it gardening, painting, reading, window shopping, tinkering with your tools, going for a walk with your spouse or friend? Is it watching an old movie or going to the beach for an hour or a whole day? It doesn't have to make sense to anyone but you. First, you must know what refreshes you and then you must make that a priority; you must work it into your schedule.

Kathryn and I recently planned a four-day getaway. We had to work hard to keep it in our schedules. At the same time, we made plans to spend our Christmas holiday with my wife's family. We had to make those plans months in advance to ensure that we could create some family memories with those who are now spread out all over our country.

It is often hard work to plan rest and recreation. Don't let these days get away from you, but take some time to have some fun or get some rest. After all, even God rested from His work on the seventh day. If God needed a break, in a manner of speaking, so do you.

ACTION PLAN: How did you do last week at scheduling something you wanted to do for yourself? Did you put an "X" on your planner so that the day was set aside? Did you keep the appointment with yourself?

Now let's go beyond this week. Look at the rest of the year and "X" out one day every week as your day off, or one night a week for that class you've talked about attending. Don't forget about holidays or family gatherings. Get those on your calendar as well, maybe even a year in advance of when they will happen. If you don't plan to have fun, you may never have any!

WEEK 47
I Broke My Own Rule!

It happened again! I had three big projects to work on, and I couldn't make up my mind which one to work on first. So I didn't do anything for quite a while. I made a few phone calls, read the news on the internet, sorted out some papers on my desk, but just couldn't get going. Finally, I forced myself to go to my daily to-do list and make a decision. It was almost too painful to decide where to begin. Everything in me wanted to give up and go watch television. That forced me to reflect on the issue of procrastination, something that plagues most people at one time or another, including you.

Why do we procrastinate? Sometimes we are lazy, pure and simple. If we aren't disciplined, and no one is forcing us to do something, we can choose to be lazy and do nothing. That probably isn't the only reason we procrastinate, however. Let's look at some other possible reasons.

One reason may be fear of failure. We are so afraid of doing the wrong thing that we choose to do nothing at all. If that is the case, a good project or idea goes undone because of fear. We may not know how to start, so we put off starting. It is like standing at a fork in the road, not knowing the right direction. So we choose neither one of them and stay where we are.

Finally, we may be convinced that we don't have the time to finish the project or enough time to do it well, so we don't even start. This is my number one reason for procrastination, and it often keeps me from starting writing projects such as reports, short articles, and even books. My thinking goes like this: *This will probably require five hours. I don't know where I'll find five hours, so why start something I can't finish?* What can *you* do to break this cycle of procrastination?

First, you can do what I did when faced with those three projects. I cheated and broke one of my own rules. I didn't work on the most important or urgent project first. I worked on one that I knew I would enjoy. I promised myself when that was done, I would move on to a more important, but boring, project. I created momentum, and it carried me into something I was putting off.

After I did the first two items, I went on to a project that wasn't even on my list, taking time to rework some notes and presentation slides with which I was not happy. When I got those done, I was so energized that I moved on to one final project I was dreading and finished that around midnight. (I did take two breaks to watch American football on television.) I overcame procrastination and got some important things done and felt great when it was all over.

Isn't it time you faced the reasons you procrastinate? Is it fear, or laziness? Are you being unrealistic, thinking you can do more than you have the time to do? Whatever it is, why not address the problem this week on your way to new levels of productivity and self-esteem?

ACTION PLAN: No matter what day of the week you are reading this, sit down with the calendar in your time-management system and plan your next seven days. Write down things you've been putting off doing, along with things you know you will enjoy doing. Plan a mix of fun things along with some that don't bring the same measure of joy. See if you can use the momentum of finishing one enjoyable task to carry you into something for which you have less enthusiasm. Then, reflect in your journal on why you procrastinate and determine to find ways to overcome this bad habit.

WEEK 48

Nancy's Story

I've told Nancy's story in my book *Unlocking The Power of Your Purpose,* and I believe it is important to include it in this book as well. A friend of our family, Nancy Gordon, attended one of the first purpose seminars I ever taught, and was impacted by the purpose message. Here's what she later e-mailed me:

> I remember hearing you teach on purpose in your "Life is a Gold Mine; Can You Dig It?" seminar. At that time I was at a critical point in my faith journey. I ached for more creative expression in my life. Being the daughter of the sports editor for our local paper, writing came naturally and easy for me. I loved words and I had always loved music.

> Little did I realize that your seminar would be one of the things God would use to help me find the courage to believe and pursue the desires of my heart, namely songwriting. First, I had to acknowledge the desire that I wanted to write to myself, to God, and to family and friends. Then I began to actively pursue this dream and desire, one day at a time, one step at a time. I remember the phrase "Never despise small beginnings." Maybe I heard it from you.

> Now some years later, I have published more than 300 songs, written twelve musicals (children and adult), have had four songs nominated for a Dove

Award, and created the children's praise character Miss PattyCake. The Miss PattyCake line now has six videos and two CDs, which I helped to write and create. I just finished my first book to be published and released in March, which will be a Miss PattyCake Easter story. There's so much more, but I don't know how much you want to hear.

As a speaker, writer, worship leader, and a creative consultant, I desire to increase my speaking venues and to write several books. I now have my own publishing company, Mother's Heart Music and Mother's Heart Ministries. They both exist to nurture, inspire and encourage all people to experience and know the love of God.

You would have to know Nancy to fully appreciate this report. She's neither wealthy, nor is she "well-connected" in the music industry. (I write this because some people place successful people in a special category, thus forfeiting the encouragement those people can provide.) She is a "regular person," like you and me, who decided one day to step out, as she says, "to actively pursue this dream and desire one day at a time, one step at a time." She gave God something to bless and He did. The exciting thing is that she isn't finished. God has more for her to do and she's still young. (She's around my age, which is looking younger all the time!)

The same is true for you. Are you ready to get started? Maybe it starts by giving yourself permission to be who you are and do what you want to do. Don't underestimate how important that is in the process of being more creative and productive.

ACTION PLAN: Like Nancy, your journey can begin this week. Your journey will start where hers did: by acknowledging to yourself, to God, and to others what you want and what you were created to do. They may laugh, they may yawn or misunderstand. Their reaction (or lack of it) isn't important because you're not saying it for them. You're saying it for yourself.

If you don't have anyone to tell this week, then send me an email as Nancy did: johnstanko@att.net.

WEEK 49
Time-Awareness Week

By now you know that Peter Drucker, who is considered by many to be the father of modern management studies, has made a big impact on my life. He has impacted the world through his books and articles on a wide variety of management and leadership topics. I've read many of his books, and Drucker taught me many things. In some ways he was, and is, my mentor, although we never spent any time together.

One of the things Drucker emphasized was how important it is to know where your time is going. He pointed out that we think we know how we spend our time, but most often we don't really know. Drucker recommended conducting a time inventory once a year to see exactly where your time is going. I took his advice and have found it to be a valuable, although somewhat awkward, exercise.

For example, one of my time inventories revealed that I was investing 14 hours per week watching television! That shocked me. I had always bragged to people that I didn't watch much television. I certainly had to make some changes when confronted with that kind of evidence! By putting some of that television time to better use, I was subsequently able to produce things that were more important to me, such as writing, studying, and reading.

Why is this important? It's important because, to be productive, you must find ways to find blocks of time that can be put to creative use. You can't write, learn, study, or build a relationship by investing minutes; you must sometimes find hours to do those things.

Maybe it's time for you to consider doing a time inventory. If you decide to do one, consider doing it for at least one week. Write down what you are doing in half-hour increments. If you spend a half hour on the phone, record that in your inventory log. If you spend two hours preparing dinner, then make a note of that. At the end of the week, you will have an accurate and revealing record of your time and where it goes. When you see where your time is going, you can make adjustments based on accurate information. I hope you will find time this week that you didn't know you had.

ACTION PLAN: Let's make this week "time-awareness" week to see if you can devote more time to things that you just can't seem to find the time to do. Does the inventory sound like it's too much or too intimidating for you to do? Then how about tracking the time you spend only on certain activities. Conduct an inventory to see how much time you spend doing certain things like watching television, sleeping, talking on the phone, commuting to work, or preparing food.

When you have your total at the end of this week, see if there is any way you can either reduce the time spent there or make that time more productive. For instance, by always having an audio book in my car, I have been able to double the number of books I read. My driving time has now been converted to learning time and I am the better for it. Your time inventory will help you to do the same.

WEEK 50
Divine Energy

As I mentioned earlier, many people ask me the secret of how I do all that I do. They receive my weekly email, *The Monday Memo*, look at my travel and speaking schedule, and wonder how I can maintain a schedule like I do. I get that question so often that I have developed a three-part answer, which I would like to share with you this week. It is based on what Paul wrote to the church at Ephesus: "I became a servant of this gospel by the gift of God's grace given me through *the working of his power*" (Ephesians 3:1-7 emphasis added).

God has given me something to do. Paul wrote that he had a special administration of God's grace. I have the same thing. I'm not portraying myself as Paul's equal, but truthfully, I have something special from God to do, build, or say, just like Paul did. You do, too. Your experience, gifts, and purpose all work together to offer something that the world has never seen before. The purpose message I have received is unique, and I want to work hard to broadcast it far and wide. You have a unique message, too. Like Paul, I'm captivated by my purpose. I cannot not do what God has assigned me to do.

I do what I do best. In other words, I focus on what I do best. After his encounter with Jesus on the Damascus road, Paul made the Gentile world his focus. Yes, he visited synagogues where Jews worshipped, but only because he knew he could find believing Gentiles there who would be open to his message. He worked efficiently, and God helped him do what he needed to do. I do what I do, in part, because I stick to what I do best, in areas where I'm most gifted. I regularly re-evaluate what I do to see if there is anything I should stop doing. I think one of the most courageous things you can do is to stop doing something, knowing there are only so many hours in a day.

I count on God's energy. Paul said that he did what he did "by the gift of God's grace given me through the *working* of his power" (emphasis added) The Greek word for working is *energeia.* It is where we get our word for energy. When you function in your purpose, there is a divine energy that works in you. You are like the burning bush that Moses saw; you burn but aren't consumed. I feel God's energy in what I do as I do it. When I don't sense that energy working, I try to determine why. That may be an indication that I need to make some adjustments.

As busy as I am, I seldom feel fatigued or overwhelmed. I think that's the way it should be. What do you have creative energy to do? Do you know? If not, then it's about time you did some self-analysis and found out.

ACTION PLAN: Take out your creativity journal and reflect on the three points I have made. First, what has God given you to do? Be as specific as you can. Second, are you doing what you do best, as often as possible? And third, do you sense God's energy in what you are doing? As you seek to answer these questions, I pray that you will recognize what gives you divine energy, and then give yourself to doing it as much as you can.

WEEK 51
Governing Values

People ask me this question all the time: "There are so many things I want to do and feel like I need to do; how do I find the time to do them?" Maybe you have also asked this question as you worked through this book. You want to be more productive, achieve your goals, and fulfill your purpose, but don't know where you'll find the time to do so. The answer lies in your ability to clarify your values, and then to allow your goals and daily tasks to flow out of your personal value system. Here is an example from my own governing values, which you can read in Appendix One.

One of my nine values is that "I am a learner." I don't want to stop learning, or else I will stop growing as a leader and person. Since learning is one of my values, I set a goal every year to read or listen to 72 books. On my prioritized daily task list, reading is a scheduled activity. In the last five years, I have read 351 books. (I know the exact number because they are all listed in my personal organizer!)

How do I find time to read? It follows this process: Learning is a value, I have a specific goal, and that goal translates into daily action. It is not something I have to labor to do, although reading that much does require some discipline. Reading, however, is also fun for me and something I genuinely look forward to every day.

On the other hand, I am not as effective at a regular exercise regimen. If you study my values, health is not a declared value on my list. Therefore exercise does not appear on my daily task list. It should, but to be honest, my lack of exercise is not a scheduling problem; it's a problem of values. I must make health something I value (and don't take for granted) before exercise will find its way onto my daily list. And if health isn't a value, then perhaps I need to understand why it isn't.

Anyone who has attended one of my seminars has probably heard me talk about values and how to identify them. Have you gone through that process? If not, then follow the action plan below.

As you know by now, there is no shortcut to being productive and self-disciplined. If you are serious about answering the question, "How do I find time to do important things?" then you must be serious about writing out the values that govern your life. Take some time to do this. You won't accomplish it in one sitting, but this is a good time to start working on it. It may seem like a tedious process, but once you do this, you'll be glad you did, and you will find yourself referring to your values over and over again.

ACTION PLAN: See Appendix One in this book to view my values and how to develop your own list. Then follow these simple steps:

- Set aside two hours.
- Identify phrases that represent values that have directed your life up to this point and phrases that represent values you wish to incorporate in your life from this point forward.
- Clarify those phrases and give them definition.
- Are any of your values harmful to you or others? Do they represent selfish or selfless behavior? You may want to eliminate any that are inconsistent with a lifestyle of love and service.

Set them in order of priority. Relax! There's no wrong way to do this. Carry them with you. Review them every six months and change them, as needed.

WEEK 52
The Way Forward

You are almost finished, but in some ways you have only just begun! Now that you have identified and clarified your values, as described in week 51, it is important that you not be content to stop there. You must take the next few steps because that is where the action is—where the rubber meets the road. Based on your values—what is important and valuable to you—you have to set some goals. We have now come full circle in this book, for we started with goals in Section One and finish with goals in Section Four.

As you know from last week, one of my values is learning, so I have determined to read at least six books every month. I also have a goal to attend one self-improvement seminar every year. Both those goals are consistent with my learning value and aren't difficult to achieve.

I have kept track of my goals in a number of different ways over the years. At this point, I keep them on index cards and carry the cards in a holder that is easy to access wherever I go. When I am on a plane or have some free time, I pull out my cards and start reviewing my goals and affirmations. I am not concerned with how or where you do it, but you must write down your goals and have them readily available to review.

Then you must take one more critical step: You must make sure that you take those goals and transfer them to specific items in your daily to-do list of your time-management system. Otherwise, your goals will remain lofty dreams and never become anything more. Reading a certain number of books a year is my goal, but I do not assume that my reading will automatically take place, so I actually write "reading" as an activity on my daily to-do list. I also put important family get-togethers and dates on my calendar up to one year in advance.

The key to goal setting is not to make the tasks "have-to-dos." If you have to force yourself to do them, then something is missing. I don't read, write, or travel because I *have to do* them, but *willingly choose to do* them. Before you set the goal, you may have to ask yourself, "Is this something that I really want to do? Is this something that I am willing to suffer for?" If the answer is yes to both questions, then you have a goal that is worthy of pursuit.

Perhaps even more important than what you will do, now that you have worked through these weekly studies, is what you will stop doing. It may not be realistic to add a goal before you make time to achieve it by eliminating something you are already doing. For instance, I could never have written *The Monday Memo* until I made room in my schedule for writing. I had to stop doing some things before I could begin writing.

Where do you want to be in five years? What do you want to be doing? Your answers of what you will do tomorrow will guide your decisions of what to do today. Armed with that and summoning the courage to say, "This is important and that is not," get busy applying what you have learned to create the life you have always wanted to live.

ACTION PLAN: With your newly defined values as a guide, it is time to decide what you want to do with your life. I recommend that you set at least one goal for every value that is on your list.

You can record your goals in your journal, but you will want to keep them in some other format so that you can carry them with you. I already mentioned that I carry my goals with me now on index cards. Find out what works for you and don't be tied to one way of doing this. You aren't interested in a format that will win an award for art; you are pursuing a life that matters.

Break down your goals into a series of tasks that can be carried out on a daily basis. I have a goal to write a commentary on every book in the New Testament. That translates into writing about four verses a day, which I have done for five years and will need to do for another four. That will enable me to write those commentaries in nine years. What can you do every day that will produce the life you've always wanted to do? I urge you to pay the price and do it. You will find, however, that it all starts and ends with goals.

AFTERWORD

Congratulations! You have finished these 52 lessons and sharpened your ability to be productive—and you're still here! That's great because the best is yet to come. Are you ready to write, paint, create, and be productive in a way that's most meaningful for you? Have you already begun?

There is no real secret to productivity. When people ask me how I write my books, I answer, "One page at a time, one day at a time." That is how I wrote this one as well. The Chinese say that the journey of a thousand miles begins with the first step. They could have added "and a lot of other steps after that first one!"

I am always delighted to help anyone on their Purpose Quest, and I am happy to help you on your Productivity Quest as well. If I can be of service to you, please let me know. In Appendix Two, you can read more about my company's services that are available to you. I look forward to hearing from you, and to enjoying the fruit of your labor as you journey toward becoming a person of purpose and productivity.

ENDNOTES

[1] *The Artist's Way*, by Julia Cameron (Penguin Putnam Inc., New York, 2002), page 7.

[2] "Fame Is a Fickle Food," by Emily Dickinson, from *The Poems of Emily Dickinson*, Ralph W. Franklin editor, The Belknap Press of Harvard University Press, © 1998, 1951, 1955, 1979

[3] *The MondayMorningMemo of Roy Williams, The Wizard of Ads*, December 26, 2005.

[4] "Failure Is the Best Medicine," by Paul Saffo, *Newsweek*, March 25, 2002

[5] *Small Is the New Big: and 183 Other Riffs, Rants, and Remarkable Business Ideas*, by Seth Godwin, (Portfolio Publishers: New York, 2006), pages 52-53.

[6] *The Seven Habits of Highly Effective People* annual calendar with quotes from Stephen R. Covey.

[7] *The Sound of Paper: Starting From Scratch*, by Julia Cameron, (Tarcher Publishers: New York, 2004), page 105.

[8] *The Wizard of Ads: Turning Words into Magic and Dreamers into Millionaires*, by Roy H. Williams (Bard Press: Austin, Texas, 1998), page 196.

[9] *On Becoming a Servant Leader: The Private Writings of Robert K. Greenleaf*, edited by Don M. Frick, Larry C. Spears (Jossey-Bass, Inc.: San Francisco, 1996), page 306.

APPENDIX 1

HOW TO DEFINE
YOUR GOVERNING VALUES

As I've studied successful leaders, I've seen that they have almost always developed an inner set of values, whether they are aware that they have or not. Each one has a set of guidelines that help them make decisions, small or great. Some have written down these values and carry them in a notebook or planner; others carry them on the "tablets of their heart." Most often these values were developed and defined from:

- Family examples, both positive and negative
- Mentoring relationships
- Religious teachings
- Life failures
- Suffering through tough times
- Watching other leaders whom they admired
- Watching other leaders whom they did not admire

For instance, some who were taken advantage of have vowed never to do the same, and others, out of the same situation, decided to take advantage of as many people as possible. Both have developed values that guide their decisions. Others have felt the pain of domineering leadership and decided to perpetuate that style; some hold the value not to rule with an iron fist, but rather with an open hand. Both have developed values. And without realizing it, you have developed some values, too.

Robert Greenleaf, in his book, *On Becoming a Servant*

Leader, stated "This is the ultimate test: What values govern one's life—at the end of it?"[9] He poses an interesting question, don't you think?

Are you developing a set of values that adjust over your lifetime as your leadership grows and matures? You shouldn't wait until you're a leader to try to define these values, for by then you may not see the importance of such a task ("I'm already a leader; why sweat the small stuff now when big decisions await?"). If you wait too long to reflect on your values, you may find you've already given your energy to values that weren't worth the effort you gave them.

As most successful leaders, the apostle Paul had a set of values that guided his ministry and ministry decisions:

• Not taking financial support from the churches he was starting

• Not working where someone had already labored to start a church

• Always visiting the synagogue first when arriving in an area

• Traveling in the company of a team

• Not insisting on a Jewish lifestyle as he visited diverse cultures and people

Paul's success wasn't a matter of chance. At least part of his success came from the fact that he had a set of values that served to guide his life and work decisions. He didn't impose these values on others, for they belonged to him, having been shaped by his own experience and understanding of what God wanted him to do.

I'm grateful to the Franklin Covey Company for helping me develop my values. When I was studying to become a certified time-management facilitator through that company, their instructor directed all those who were being trained to write out our values. He told us there weren't a maximum or minimum number, and he encouraged us to write them in a positive style that related to the present ("I am"), and not the future ("I will"). Then he asked that we attempt to prioritize those values and, from that point forward, carry them with us for regular review and adjustment.

The company's objective was to allow us to see our values and allow them to better guide our decisions, decisions we would be making as leaders. In fact, they called these values our governing values, since they do (sometimes without realizing it) govern our life and decisions. This has been a most rewarding experience. I now regularly work with other leaders and potential leaders to help them develop a set of values that will guide (or are guiding) their life and leadership.

I offer my own values as an example of how they can be done, not as a model list of values to be held. I developed mine by identifying my favorite passages from the Bible. I then did what the Franklin Covey Company asked me to do: I put some narrative explanation to each value and prioritized them.

Developing values, however, isn't a science with rigid rules and procedures; rather it's an art. At the end of my list, I'll make some further recommendations of how to develop your list of governing values. Keep in mind that mine are based on a Christian life and worldview and aren't offered with anything in mind except to give you a better understanding of my leadership style, and what up-to-date, prioritized governing values can look like.

GOVERNING VALUES
FOR DR. JOHN W. STANKO
(Updated October 2006)

1. I do the will of God.

I prayed one time that I would be like Timothy, not fully realizing what I was praying. I saw Timothy in an entirely new light as I read Philippians 2:19-23:

> *I hope in the Lord Jesus to send Timothy to you soon, that I also may be cheered when I receive news about you. I have no one else like him, who takes a genuine interest in your welfare. For everyone looks out for his own interests and not those of Jesus Christ. But you know that Timothy has proved himself, because as a son with his father he has served with me in the work of the gospel. I hope, therefore, to send him as soon as I see how things go with me.*

The will of God, as I understand it, is to put other's interests before my own and to serve in furthering the gospel as the Holy Spirit and my oversight so direct. That also involves a vibrant and diligent prayer and study life that seeks to find the will of God and do it.

2. I walk in faith.

The writer of Hebrews wrote, "Without faith it is impossible to please God." I want to please the Lord by exercising faith in Him concerning my purpose, family, finances, future, and relationships. The second part of that verse completes the thought when it says, "because anyone who comes to him must believe that he exists and that he rewards those who earnestly seek him" (Hebrews 11:6).

My faith will have practical expression through my giving habits as I'm generous with my time, knowledge, wisdom, and money.

3. I love my family.

The Lord has given me three wonderful gifts: Kathryn, John, and Deborah. The apostle Paul commanded husbands:

> *Love your wives, just as Christ loved the church and gave himself for her to make her holy, cleansing her by the washing with water through the word, and to present her to himself as a radiant church, without stain or wrinkle or any other blemish, but holy and blameless. In the same way, husbands ought to love their wives as their own bodies* (Ephesians 5:25-28).

I want to love my wife and see her released to her purpose as a joint heir with me of the gracious gift of life (1 Peter 3:7).

He also told fathers not to "embitter your children, or they will become discouraged" (Colossians 3:21). I want to be a friend and encourager to my children and release them to their God-given purpose.

4. I am a servant-leader.

Because I am a man of purpose, I have a desire to express my purpose by serving the world in some capacity. Since my childhood, I've also found myself in leadership positions. Thus I want to combine those two roles—servant and leader—to be a servant-leader from a biblical perspective. I want to lead and serve according to God's will and implement my decisions in the right spirit and attitude. Peter wrote,

> Be shepherds of God's flock that is under your care, serving as overseers—not because you must, but because you are willing, as God wants you to be; not greedy for money, but eager to serve; not lording it over those entrusted to you, but being examples to the flock (1 Peter 5:2-3).

I want to lead in the tradition of Jesus, Moses, Joseph, David, Solomon and Daniel. I want to grow in my understanding of servant leadership, learning to listen well and to influence—not control—others. I also want to be a leader of integrity and courage.

5. I am a communicator.

Jesus was a great communicator. Mark reported that "the large crowd listened to him [Jesus] with delight" (Mark 12:37). That came from His insight into the Word, His love for people, and His effective speaking style. I want to follow in His footsteps. Jesus also said, "The Father who sent me commanded me what to say and how to say it" (John 12:49).

I want to have something to say and then know how to present it with clarity, humor, and conviction, whether speaking, writing books and articles, or communicating through other media. I also want to study and effectively utilize humor to enhance my ability to communicate with others. I acknowledge, too, that I have a sense of humor that is God-given and I am committed to use it to the glory of God.

140

6. I am energetic.

"I became a servant of this gospel by the gift of God's grace given me through the working of his power" (Ephesians 3:7).

Paul accomplished his life purpose "through the working of his [God's] power." The Greek word for working is energeia. I want to have and use this same energeia in my life and not be found working in my own strength. I will maintain this energy by staying focused on my purpose, eating healthy food, and getting appropriate rest. I will use this energy to produce more than I consume and to engage in activities that will bring increase and glory to God.

When I work, I work and walk in the truth of what Paul wrote to the Corinthians:

But by the grace of God I am what I am, and His grace toward me did not prove vain; but I labored even more than all of them, yet not I, but the grace of God with me (1 Corinthians 15:10 NAS).

7. I am a learner.

Because the world is changing so rapidly, I can't afford to "crystallize" in my work habits or thinking. That means that I must continue to learn and grow in the knowledge of God (see Colossians 1:10). My primary focus must be the word of God, and my prayer is, "Open my eyes that I may see wonderful things in your law" (Psalm 119:18). Paul wrote, "All Scripture is God-breathed and is useful for teaching, rebuking, correcting and training in righteousness, so that the man of God may be thoroughly equipped for every good work" (2 Timothy 3:16).

I'll read, study, take classes, attend seminars, learn from role models, and master new techniques and technology that will enable me to learn until my strength fails or I die.

8. *I am a reconciler.*
The gospel of Jesus Christ is the only answer to society's problems, and that includes racism. I offer myself to work with people of color and of various cultures to model relationships that will help reconcile people to God and then to one another. As Paul wrote in 2 Corinthians 5:18-20:

> *All this is from God, who reconciled us to himself through Christ and gave us the ministry of reconciliation; that God was reconciling the world to himself in Christ, not counting men's sins against them. And he has committed to us the message of reconciliation. We are therefore Christ's ambassadors, as though God were making his appeal through us. We implore you on Christ's behalf: Be reconciled to God.*

I want to mentor young men and women to equip them to be all that they can be in God and affirm their beauty and worth in God's eyes.

9. *I am a team player.*
I've been an avid sports fan since my youth. I now realize that this was simply a love for the team concept that's so vital to, yet so absent from, much of management and ministry today. I want to help others identify their life's purpose and then train and coach them to work with other people of purpose. I'll try to pursue the synergy that comes from teamwork when everyone has a chance to communicate and share their creativity in an open atmosphere as free from authoritarian techniques as possible.

The apostle Paul almost always traveled in a team and was released into ministry from the context of "team" in Acts 13:1-3:

> In the church at Antioch there were prophets and teachers: Barnabas, Simeon called Niger, Lucius of Cyrene, Manaen (who had been brought up with Herod the tetrarch), and Saul. While they were worshiping the Lord and fasting, the Holy Spirit said, "Set apart for me Barnabas and Saul for the work to which I have called them." So after they had fasted and prayed, they placed their hands on them and sent them off.

I realize that stating these values in the "I am" style may seem a bit presumptuous or arrogant. I'm not everything that I've written above. But I'm striving to embody those values, and that keeps me humble and always seeking, two traits that are, frankly, missing in many leaders today. I can never say I've arrived for that could cause me to take shortcuts or expect certain privileges that could lead to defective leadership.

Now how about you? Are you ready to spell out your governing values? Here are some other sample values that I've borrowed from Franklin Covey to help you get started:

I seek excellence.
I am competent.
I serve others.
I am frugal.
I am generous.
I seek truth.
I am self-sufficient.
I am innovative.

APPENDIX 2

READY FOR MORE?

JOHN STANKO'S SERVICES TO ASSIST YOU IN YOUR PRODUCTIVITY QUEST

I offer several services to help you be more purposeful and productive.

The first is entitled The PurposeAssessment. It consists of a one-on-one meeting with me to go over your purpose and productivity goals (in person or by phone). To enhance the process and as part of your personal development (remember Section Three), I administer three personality style profiles that come with three reports, providing invaluable information about who you are along with your optimum work style. You can contact me at johnstanko@att.net for more information.

The second is entitled The Seven Steps of a PurposeQuest. To help you understand that program, I have included a list of frequently asked questions along with my responses.

Frequently Asked Questions

Q: What resources will I receive to help me complete the Seven Steps of a PurposeQuest?

A: You will receive a set of seven CD-ROMS that cover The Seven Steps of a PurposeQuest. Along with the CDs, you will receive a notebook filled with supportive material to help you understand each of the seven steps.

Q: What are the seven steps?

A: In the program you will study purpose, values, goals, time management, servant leadership, faith and joy. Each step has one CD with a 60-minute message along with case studies, outlines and articles to read and study.

Q: What if I live outside the United States?

A: PurposeQuest International will still send you the materials. If you enroll as a Purpose Partner, I will work out an agreement with you to facilitate your personal contact with me, although distance and cost may prohibit monthly contact. In that case, I will work out a schedule with you.

Q: What can I expect at the end of the Seven Steps Program?

A: If you go through all seven steps, I'm confident that you will be a more purposeful leader, equipped to recognize your purpose when it appears. You may wish to continue your relationship with me at the end of your seven-step program.

Q: I want to help others clarify their purpose and be more productive. What do you have that can help me?

A: First, you must be familiar with the Seven Steps, so that is where you must begin. I also have a program to certify you as a PurposeQuest counselor. In the meantime, you may also wish to become certified to administer the DISC, TEAMS and Values profiles. This curriculum is available through PurposeQuest International. Write for more information on the cost of the DISC certification.

Q: What should I do if I wish to enroll?

A: You can call me at (412) 242-6506 or (877) 828-6464 (toll free) and we can discuss your enrollment in the program. If you cannot call, then email me at johnstanko@att.net.

Don't wait. Invest in yourself and contact me today!

About the Author

John has served as an administrator, teacher, consultant, author, and pastor. He earned a master's degree in economics and one in pastoral ministries, and a doctorate in pastoral ministries.

As executive director of Worship International from 1993-1995, he organized worship conferences for Integrity Music around the world, and later became a Certified Meeting Professional (CMP), the highest distinction awarded in the conference management industry. He has taught extensively on the topics of time management, life purpose and organization, and has conducted leadership and purpose training sessions throughout the United States and in 25 countries.

Recently his clients have included Integrity Music, Kabul University in Afghanistan, Lippo Bank and Lippo Land in Indonesia, Regent University in Virginia Beach, DHL in southern Africa, Kingdom Bank in Zimbabwe, the South African Regional Poverty Network in Pretoria, Celebration Ministries International in Zimbabwe and many other churches and nonprofit organizations in the United States and abroad.

FOR MORE INFORMATION CONTACT:
John W. Stanko
PurposeQuest International
P.O. Box 91099
Pittsburgh, PA 15221-7099, USA
(412) 242-4448 phone
(877) 828-6464 toll-free
(412) 242-6506 fax
johnstanko@att.net
www.purposequest.com
www.johnstanko.us (blog)